HARCOURT

Math

Problem Solving and Reading Strategies Workbook

Grade 2

Harcourt

Orlando   Austin   Chicago   New York   Toronto   London   San Diego

Visit *The Learning Site!*
www.harcourtschool.com

Printed in the United States of America

ISBN 0-15-336523-4   ISBN 978-0-15-336523-2

10 11 12 13 14 0982 13 12 11
4500338616

CONTENTS

Tens

Solve.

1. Meg counted 20 beetles in the woods. How many groups of ten beetles did she count?

   _____ groups of ten

2. Maya saw 40 caterpillars on her lawn. How many groups of ten caterpillars did she see?

   _____ groups of ten

3. Terry has an ant farm with 100 ants. How many groups of ten ants does he have?

   _____ groups of ten

4. Kwan counts 50 fireflies. How many groups of ten fireflies does he count?

   _____ groups of ten

5. How many grasshoppers does it take to make 6 groups of ten?

   _____ grasshoppers

6. How many honey bees does it take to make 9 groups of ten?

   _____ honey bees

Mark the correct answer.

7. Ethan saw 40 butterflies in the garden. How many groups of ten butterflies did he see?

   ○ 2 groups of ten

   ○ 4 groups of ten

   ○ 20 groups of ten

   ○ 40 groups of ten

8. Tate has 3 bags of seeds. Each bag has 10 seeds. How many seeds does she have?

   ○ 3 seeds

   ○ 10 seeds

   ○ 15 seeds

   ○ 30 seeds

Name _____

Tens and Ones

Draw a model. Then solve.

1. Julie puts her rocks in 1 group of ten. She has 6 rocks left over. How many rocks does she have?

   __16__ rocks

2. Nick puts his stickers in 6 groups of ten. He has 7 left over. How many stickers does he have?

   _____ stickers

3. Josh puts his cars in 3 groups of ten. He has 3 cars left over. How many cars does he have?

   _____ cars

Mark the correct answer.

4. Which is the number?

   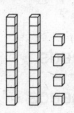

   ○ 20   ○ 24

   ○ 40   ○ 42

5. Which number is the same as 40 + 9?

   ○ 40   ○ 44

   ○ 49   ○ 94

PS2   Problem Solving

Name _____

Understand Place Value

Solve.

1. Scott sorted his marbles into 5 groups of ten. He had 3 marbles left over. How many marbles did Scott have?

   _____ marbles

2. Kari made 3 stacks of blocks. Each stack had 10 blocks. How many blocks did she stack?

   _____ blocks

3. Marty had 73 bricks. He put them in stacks of ten. How many bricks did Marty stack?

   _____ bricks

4. Sally wrote the number 27 on a piece of paper. What is the value of the digit 2 in the number?

   _____

5. Tony saw a number on a sign. The number had 5 ones and 8 tens. What was the number Tony saw?

   _____

6. Han thought of a number. She said her number had 2 tens and 3 ones. What was the number?

   _____

Mark the correct answer.

7. What is the value of the underlined digit?

   3<u>5</u>

   ○ 3
   ○ 5
   ○ 30
   ○ 50

8. What is the value of the underlined digit?

   8<u>3</u>

   ○ 3
   ○ 8
   ○ 30
   ○ 80

Name _____

Read and Write Numbers to 100

Write the number three different ways.

1. Mr. Torres has 5 boxes with 10 books in each. He buys 3 more books. How many books does he have in all?

__5__ tens __3__ ones

____ + ____

____ books

2. Ms. Francis has 7 boxes with 10 books in each. She buys 6 more books. How many books does she have in all?

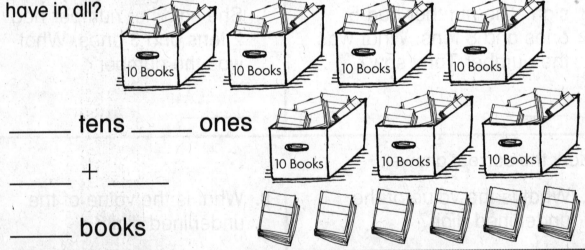

____ tens ____ ones

____ + ____

____ books

Mark the correct answer.

3. Which number has 2 tens and 8 ones?

⚬ 73   ⚬ 47

⚬ 28   ⚬ 19

4. Which number is the same as 60 + 7?

⚬ 32   ⚬ 67

⚬ 77   ⚬ 83

Understand **Plan** **Solve** **Check**

Algebra: Different Ways to Show Numbers

Solve.
Circle the answer.

1. Pam wrote the number 74 on the board. What is another way she could have written the number?

7 tens 4 ones   40 + 7

2. Len wrote 2 tens 8 ones on a piece of paper. What is another way Len could have written the number?

80 + 2   28

3. Lisa used tens and ones to show 36. How did Lisa show the number?

4. Mike drew a picture to show 15. Which picture did Mike draw?

5. José wrote the number 25 in a place value chart. Which chart did he use?

tens	ones

tens	ones

6. Suni wrote 10 + 8 on the board. What is another way she could have shown the number?

8 tens 1 one

tens	ones

Mark the correct answer.

7. What is another way to show 76?

○ 7 + 60

○ 6 tens 7 ones

○ 70 + 6

○ 7 tens 7 ones

8. What is another way to show 41?

○ 10 + 4

○ 4 tens 1 one

○ 4 tens 4 ones

○ 40 + 4

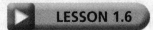

Reading Strategy • Create Mental Images

Picture the estimates in your mind.
Then circle the most reasonable estimate.

1. James has some cats.
About how many cats might
he have?

(**3**)   30   100

2. Shelby has these pencils in a
box. About how many pencils
might be in the box?

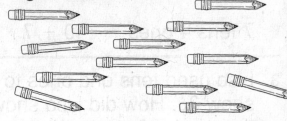

2   20   100

3. Dan gives each of his
classmates a card. About how
many cards might that be?

3   30   100

4. Maria counts buttons on her
shirt. About how many buttons
might be on her shirt?

7   50   100

5. Todd fills a large bag with toy
rings. About how many rings
might be in the bag?

8   20   100

6. Lani returns books to the
library. About how many books
might she have returned?

6   60   100

Algebra: Counting on a Number Line

Solve. Use the number line to help you.

1.
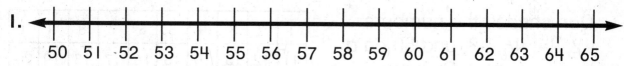

Wasaki started on number 54.
He counted forward 8 jumps.
To what number did he count? _____

2.
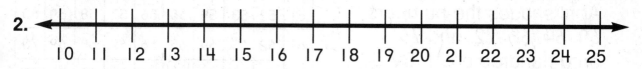

Kaya started on number 17.
She counted backward 5 jumps.
To what number did she count? _____

3.

Darnell started on number 32.
He counted backward 6 jumps.
To what number did he count? _____

Use the number line.
Mark the correct answer.

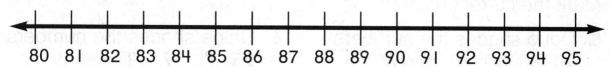

4. Start on 83. Count forward 7. To what number do you count?

○ 89   ○ 90

○ 91   ○ 92

5. Start on 92. Count backward 5. To what number do you count?

○ 89   ○ 88

○ 87   ○ 86

Algebra: Hundred Chart and Skip-Counting Patterns

Solve. Use the hundred chart to help you.

1. Dan shades the numbers 42, 44, 46, 48, and 50 on a hundred chart. By what number is he skip-counting?

_____

1	2	3	4	5	6	7	8	9	10
11	12	13	14	15	16	17	18	19	20
21	22	23	24	25	26	27	28	29	30
31	32	33	34	35	36	37	38	39	40
41	42	43	44	45	46	47	48	49	50
51	52	53	54	55	56	57	58	59	60
61	62	63	64	65	66	67	68	69	70
71	72	73	74	75	76	77	78	79	80
81	82	83	84	85	86	87	88	89	90
91	92	93	94	95	96	97	98	99	100

2. April shades the numbers 60, 64, 68, 72, and 76 on a hundred chart. By what number is she skip-counting?

_____

3. Alyssa shades the numbers 65, 70, 75, 80, and 85 on a hundred chart. She continues the pattern. What is the next number Alyssa shades?

_____

4. Emma shades the numbers 30, 33, 36, 39, and 42 on a hundred chart. She continues the pattern. What is the next number Emma shades?

_____

Mark the correct answer.

5. Doug shades the numbers 20, 30, 40, 50, and 60 on a hundred chart. By what number is he skip-counting?

○ 4   ○ 5
○ 8   ○ 10

6. Chloe shades the numbers 25, 31, 37, 43, and 49 on a hundred chart. She continues the pattern. What is the next number Chloe shades?

○ 52   ○ 53
○ 54   ○ 55

Even and Odd

Solve. Use 🎲 to help.
Write **even** or **odd**.

1. Caleb has 8 cubes and Kito
   has 6 cubes. Do they have an
   even or an odd number of cubes?   _____

2. Haley has 15 cubes and Jordan
   has 21 cubes. Do they have an
   even or an odd number of cubes?   _____

3. Asha has 14 cubes and José has
   19 cubes. Do they have an even or
   an odd number of cubes?   _____

4. Jina has 8 cubes and Shani has
   18 cubes. Do they have an even
   or an odd number of cubes?   _____

5. Jiro has 7 cubes and Cole has
   10 cubes. Do they have an even
   or an odd number of cubes?   _____

Mark the correct answer.

6. Which number is odd?

   ○ 34
   ○ 66
   ○ 48
   ○ 87

7. Which number is even?

   ○ 27
   ○ 73
   ○ 56
   ○ 95

Understand Plan Solve Check

Reading Strategy: Make Predictions

Sometimes a problem asks you to tell
what will happen next.

Mark wants to fill up his photo album.
Each page holds 3 pictures. There are
6 pages. How many pictures will Mark use?

Make a chart. Look for a pattern.

number of pages	1	2	3	4	5	6
number of pictures	3	6	9	12	15	18

1. What is the pattern? _____add 3_____

2. How many pictures do 6 pages hold? _____18_____

3. Mark will use _____18_____ pictures.

_____

Use the chart to figure out what will happen.
Then solve.

4. 4 skateboarders are putting on
   knee and elbow pads. How many
   pads will they use in all?

skateboarders	1	2	3	4
number of pads	4			

What is the pattern? _____

How many pads do 4 skateboarders need? _____ pads

The skateboarders will use _____ pads.

Understand Plan Solve Check

Ordinal Numbers

Solve.

1. Tami is seventh in line.
Mia is just behind her.
In what position is Mia?

_____

2. Adam is on the 5th floor.
He walks up to the next floor.
What floor is he on now?

_____

3. Irene is third in line.
Nick is just in front of her.
In what position is Nick?

_____

4. Avi is 9th in line.
Kara is just behind him.
In what position is Kara?

_____

5. There are 15 cars in line.
A green car is last. A blue
car is just in front of the
green car. In what position
is the blue car?

_____

6. Lamar finishes second in a
race. He crosses the finish
line just behind Kurt. In what
position is Kurt?

_____

Mark the correct answer.

7. I am just after the 12th
person in line. What is
my position?

○ 10th

○ 13th

○ 11th

○ 14th

8. I am just before the eighth
person in line. What is
my position?

○ 7th

○ 10th

○ 9th

○ 12th

Understand | Plan | Solve | Check

Algebra: Compare Numbers: >, <, or =

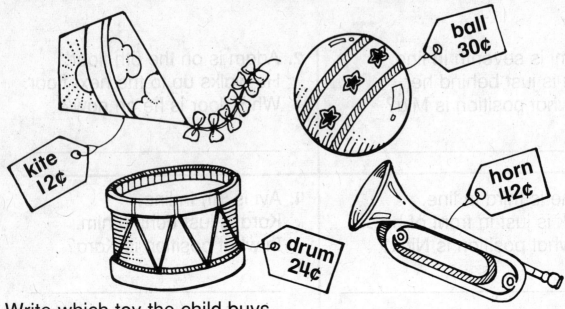

Write which toy the child buys.

1. Tom buys a toy. The price of the toy is greater than 35¢. _____horn_____	**2.** Jessie buys a toy. The price of the toy is less than 15¢. _____
3. Matt buys a toy. The price of the toy is greater than 25¢ and less than 35¢. _____	**4.** Becky buys a toy. The price of the toy is greater than 20¢ and less than 25¢. _____

Mark the correct answer.

5. Choose >, <, or =.

27 ◯ 19

◯ <
◯ >
◯ =

6. Choose >, <, or =.

46 ◯ 64

◯ <
◯ >
◯ =

Order Numbers to 100

Solve.

1. Mary numbered her problems 10, 11, 13, 14, and 15. What number did she leave out?

   _____

2. David is putting number blocks in order. He lines up blocks 31, 32, and 33. What block is next?

   _____

3. Joe's house is between two houses numbered 63 and 65. What is the number of Joe's house?

   _____

4. There are three lockers. The first one is number 23. The last one is number 25. What is the number of the locker between 23 and 25?

   _____

5. Tara likes to count backward. She counts 12, 11, 9, 8. What number did Tara leave out?

   _____

6. Jerry is counting down for the race. He counts 5, 4, 3, 1. What number did Jerry leave out?

   _____

Mark the correct answer.

7. 15, _____, 17, 18

   ○ 12

   ○ 13

   ○ 14

   ○ 16

8. 28, 29, _____, 31

   ○ 26

   ○ 27

   ○ 30

   ○ 32

Understand   Plan   Solve   Check

10 More, 10 Less

Solve.

1. Nari counts 12 birds.
Josh counts 10 more than
Nari. How many birds does
Josh count?

_____ birds

2. Rico saved 65¢.
Chris saved 10¢ less.
How much did Chris save?

_____ ¢

3. Tony swims for 33 minutes.
Lita swims 10 minutes longer.
How many minutes does
Lita swim?

_____ minutes

4. Mark buys 15 marbles.
Jack buys 10 fewer marbles.
How many marbles does
Jack buy?

_____ marbles

5. Kate's class has 29 students.
Ruth's class has 10 fewer
students. How many students
does Ruth's class have?

_____ students

6. Dena has 6 markers.
She gets 10 more.
How many markers does
Dena have now?

_____ markers

Mark the correct answer.

7. What number is 10 more
than 53?

○ 43

○ 52

○ 54

○ 63

8. What number is 10 less
than 71?

○ 17

○ 61

○ 70

○ 81

Name _____

Reading Strategy • Create Mental Images

Jake has 19 books.
About how many books does he have?
Round to the nearest ten.

Picture the problem.

Choose a way to solve the problem.   Make a model.
Draw a picture.

Solve.

```
←——+——+——+——+——+——+——+——+——+——+——+——→
   10  11  12  13  14  15  16  17  18 (19) 20
```

19 is closer to __20__ than to __10__.

Jack has about __20__ books.

Picture the problems.
Then solve.

1. Mai has 32 pennies.
Does she have about 30
or about 40 pennies?

32 is closer to __30__

Mai has about __30__
pennies.

2. Del has 48 markers.
Does she have about 40
or about 50 markers?

48 is closer to _____

Del has about _____
markers.

3. Dan walks 14 blocks.
Does he walk about 10
or about 20 blocks?

14 is closer to _____

Dan walks about _____
blocks.

4. Ho rides his bicycle for
28 minutes. Does he
ride for about 20 or about
30 minutes?

28 is closer to _____

Ho rides for about _____
minutes.

Name _____

Take a Survey on a Tally Table

The tally table shows the favorite sports of the children in Mr. Kim's class.

Favorite Sport	
Sport	**Tally**
Swimming	卌 ||
Biking	卌 卌
Rollerblading	||||
Running	|||

Use the table to solve.

1. How many children like rollerblading best?

_____ children

2. Which sport do 7 children like best?

_____

3. Which sport do the most children like best?

_____

4. Which sport do the fewest children like best?

_____

5. How many more children chose biking than swimming?

_____ children

6. How many more children chose swimming than running?

_____ children

Mark the correct answer.

7. How many fewer children chose rollerblading than biking?

○ 6   ○ 4

○ 5   ○ 3

8. How many fewer children chose swimming than biking?

○ 6   ○ 4

○ 5   ○ 3

PS16   Problem Solving

Use Data in Tables

Jan took a survey. She asked children in her group to name their favorite season. Then she asked her whole class the same question.

Favorite Season for Jan's Group	
Season	**Tally**
Winter	||
Spring		
Summer	|||||
Fall		

Favorite Season for Jan's Class	
Season	**Tally**
Winter	|||
Spring	||||
Summer	||||| ||||| ||||
Fall	||

Use the tally tables to solve.

1. How many children in Jan's group like spring best?

_____

2. How many children in Jan's class like winter best?

_____

3. How many children in the group like fall or winter best?

_____

4. How many children in the class like spring or summer best?

_____

Mark the correct answer.

5. Which season is the favorite in Jan's class?

○ winter   ○ spring

○ summer   ○ fall

6. Which season is the favorite of 2 children in the group?

○ winter   ○ spring

○ summer   ○ fall

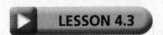

  Solve

Make a Concrete Graph

The children in Mr. Bozak's class collected leaves. They made a concrete graph to show what trees the leaves came from.

		Leaves We Found							

Kinds of Leaves

Oak	🍂	🍂	🍂	🍂	🍂			
Maple	🍁	🍁	🍁	🍁	🍁	🍁	🍁	🍁
Birch	🍃	🍃	🍃					

Number of Leaves

Use the graph to solve.

1. How many oak leaves did the class find?

_____ oak leaves

2. How many maple leaves did the class find?

_____ maple leaves

3. Did the class find more oak leaves or more birch leaves?

_____ leaves

4. Did the class find more birch leaves or more maple leaves?

_____ leaves

Mark the correct answer.

5. How many leaves did the class find that were not oak leaves?

○ 8   ○ 11

○ 13   ○ 16

6. How many leaves did the class find in all?

○ 8   ○ 11

○ 13   ○ 16

Make a Pictograph

Ways Classmates Traveled Last Month				
☺				
☺				☺
☺				☺
☺	☺			☺
☺	☺	☺		☺
Car	Truck	Train	Airplane	Bus

Key: Each ☺ stands for 5 children.

Use the graph to solve.

1. How many classmates rode in a truck last month?

_____

2. How many classmates rode in an airplane?

_____

3. What did 20 classmates travel in last month?

_____

4. How many more classmates rode in a truck than in a train?

_____

Solve. Use the graph. Mark the best answer.

5. In what did the most classmates travel last month?

○ bus   ○ train

○ car   ○ truck

6. In what did the fewest classmates travel last month?

○ airplane   ○ train

○ car   ○ truck

Name _____

Reading Strategy • Use Graphic Aids

Chen saw this graph in a book. He used the graph to answer a question.

If the zoo gets two more lions, how many lions will it have?

_____4_____ lions

Animals at the Zoo			
	ZOO		
	ZOO		
	ZOO	ZOO	
	ZOO	ZOO	ZOO
ZOO	ZOO	ZOO	ZOO
Lions	**Monkeys**	**Bears**	**Elephants**

Key: Each ZOO stands for 2 animals.

Use the graph to solve.

1. How many animals does each ZOO stand for?

_____

2. How many animals does the graph show in all?

_____ animals

3. Of which animal does the zoo have the least?

_____

4. Of which animal does the zoo have the most?

_____

5. The zoo wants to get two more elephants. How many elephants will it have then?

_____ elephants

6. The zoo is going to give 4 monkeys to another zoo. How many monkeys will it have left?

_____ monkeys

PS20 Reading Strategy

Count On

Count on to find the sum.

1. There are 6 kites in the air. There are 2 kites on the ground. How many kites are there?

$6 + 2 =$ __8__ kites

2. Joyce had 5 crayons. Larry gave her 1 crayon. How many crayons does Joyce have now?

$5 + 1 =$ _____ crayons

3. Gary drew 4 pictures. Then he drew 2 more. How many pictures did Gary draw?

$4 + 2 =$ _____ pictures

4. There are 9 girls. There are 3 boys. How many children are there?

$9 + 3 =$ _____ children

Mark the correct answer.

5. Bella has 7 red pencils and 2 white pencils. How many pencils does Bella have?

○ 7
○ 9
○ 10
○ 11

6. There are 10 small cats and 2 large cats. How many cats are there?

○ 2
○ 8
○ 10
○ 12

Name _____

Doubles and Doubles Plus One

Draw a picture.
Solve.

1. Sue has 6 green apples and 7 red apples. How many apples does she have? ____13____ apples	
2. Ian has 3 dimes. Erika has 1 more dime than Ian. How many dimes do they have together? _____ dimes	
3. 5 people ride in a red car and 5 people ride in a green car. How many people ride in all? _____ people	
4. Amy collects 8 shells. Then she collects 9 more. How many shells does she collect? _____ shells	

Mark the correct answer.

5. Which is 1 more than 7 + 7?

- ○ 7 + 6
- ○ 7 + 8
- ○ 8 + 8
- ○ 8 + 9

6. Which is 1 less than 6 + 6?

- ○ 7 + 7
- ○ 6 + 7
- ○ 6 + 5
- ○ 5 + 5

Make a Ten

Understand   Plan   Solve   Check

Draw ○. Make a ten. Write the sum.

1. Mr. Long bought 8 red apples and 5 green apples. How many apples did he buy? ___13___ apples	
2. Ted sees 6 red hens and 9 white hens. How many hens does he see? _____ hens	
3. Julie has 9 toy horses. She gets 4 more. How many horses does Julie have? _____ horses	
4. Ryan has 4 dogs and 7 cats. How many pets does Ryan have? _____ pets	

Mark the correct answer.

5. Jo has 7 dolls. Su has 6 more dolls than Jo. How many dolls does Su have?
   - ○ 15
   - ○ 14
   - ○ 13
   - ○ 12

6. Larry read 8 books. Ken read 6 more books than Larry. How many books did Ken read?
   - ○ 14
   - ○ 15
   - ○ 16
   - ○ 17

Name _____

 Understand Plan Solve Check

Algebra: Add 3 Numbers

Draw a picture. Then write the number sentence.

1. Lin has 3 red fish, 4 blue fish, and 5 yellow fish. How many fish does Lin have?

$\underline{3} + \underline{4} + \underline{5} = \underline{12}$ fish

2. Charlie has 3 blue boats, 2 red boats, and 3 yellow boats. How many boats does he have?

___ + ___ + ___ = _____ boats

3. Jason has 8 boats. He has 9 more rafts than boats. How many rafts does he have?

___ + ___ = _____ rafts

4. Kali has 5 big fish and 6 little fish. How many fish does she have?

___ + ___ = _____ fish

Mark the correct answer.

5. Ron has 1 red car, 4 green cars, and 5 blue cars. How many cars does he have?

○ 9   ○ 11

○ 10   ○ 12

6. Lisa sees 2 white birds, 4 black birds, and 3 brown birds. How many birds does she see?

○ 6   ○ 8

○ 7   ○ 9

Name _____

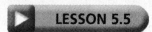

Understand Plan Solve Check

Reading Strategy • Use Picture Clues

Using picture clues can help
you solve problems.

Read the problem. Use picture
clues to help you solve it.

There are ___3___ crabs in the water.

There are _____ crabs in the sand.

There are _____ crabs on a rock.

How many crabs are there in all? _____ crabs

Look for picture clues.
Solve the problems.

1. Jake saw _____ turtles at

   the beach. He saw _____

   starfish. He saw _____ seagulls.

   How many animals did

   Jake see in all?

   _____ animals

---

2. Ruby found _____ shells.

   Sara found _____ shells.

   Molly found _____ shells.

   How many shells

   did they find in all?

   _____ shells

Reading Strategy   PS25

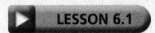

Count Back

Write the number sentence.

1. Raj had 8 carrot sticks.
He ate 2 of them.
How many carrot sticks
did Raj have left?

$\underline{8} - \underline{2} = \underline{6}$

carrot sticks

2. Nina had 10 golf balls.
She lost 1 of them.
How many golf balls
did Nina have left?

___ − ___ = ___

golf balls

3. Ivan and Kim made a tower
with 11 blocks. The top
3 blocks fell off. How many
blocks were left in the tower?

___ − ___ = ___

blocks

4. Tina has 9 bags of popcorn.
There are 3 large bags. The
rest are small bags. How
many small bags does Tina
have?

___ − ___ = ___

small bags

5. The rose bush has 6 flowers.
Alana picks 2 of them. How
many roses are left on the
bush?

___ − ___ = ___

roses

6. There are 7 kittens playing.
Then 3 of them run to their
mother. How many kittens are
still playing?

___ − ___ = ___

kittens

Mark the correct answer.

7. Roy had 10 toy cars. He gave
away 3. How many toy cars
did he have left?

○ 3   ○ 7

○ 4   ○ 8

8. There are 12 birds on the roof.
Then 2 of them fly away. How
many birds are left?

○ 9   ○ 11

○ 10   ○ 12

Algebra: Fact Families

Write the fact family for the set of numbers.

1. Martha pulls 15 cubes out of a bag.
   7 cubes are red and 8 cubes are blue.

$$\underline{7} + \underline{8} = \underline{15} \qquad \underline{8} + \underline{7} = \underline{15}$$

$$\underline{15} - \underline{7} = \underline{8} \qquad \underline{15} - \underline{8} = \underline{7}$$

2. Ann Lee pulls 11 cubes out of a bag.
   5 cubes are yellow and 6 cubes are green.

$$\underline{} + \underline{} = \underline{} \qquad \underline{} + \underline{} = \underline{}$$

$$\underline{} - \underline{} = \underline{} \qquad \underline{} - \underline{} = \underline{}$$

3. Carol pulls 17 cubes out of a bag.
   9 cubes are blue and 8 cubes are red.

$$\underline{} + \underline{} = \underline{} \qquad \underline{} + \underline{} = \underline{}$$

$$\underline{} - \underline{} = \underline{} \qquad \underline{} - \underline{} = \underline{}$$

Mark the correct answer.

4. Lin has 9 pennies. Leslie gives her 4 more. How many pennies does Lin have?

   ○ 5
   ○ 7
   ○ 13
   ○ 14

5. Which belongs in the fact family for the set of numbers?

4	5	9

   ○ $9 - 4 = 5$
   ○ $5 + 9 = 14$
   ○ $14 - 5 = 9$
   ○ $5 - 4 = 1$

Name _____

Relate Addition to Subtraction

Solve.

1. There are 7 flowers in Conor's garden. He plants 4 more. How many flowers does Conor have now?

___ + ___ = ___ flowers

2. Becky has 11 flowers. She gives 4 of them away. How many flowers does Becky have left?

___ − ___ = ___ flowers

3. Tomi bakes 8 pies. Then he bakes 5 more pies. How many pies does Tomi have in all?

___ + ___ = ___ pies

4. Lea bakes 13 pies. She gives 5 of them away. How many pies does Lea still have?

___ − ___ = ___ pies

5. There are 6 people in the room. Then 4 more people come in. How many people are in the room now?

___ + ___ = ___ people

6. There are 10 people in the room. Then 4 of them leave. How many people are in the room now?

___ − ___ = ___ people

Mark the correct answer.

7. Alana has 6 apples. She picks 5 more apples. How many apples does Alana have now?

○ 5   ○ 10
○ 6   ○ 11

8. Greg has 11 apples. He uses 5 apples to make applesauce. How many apples are left?

○ 5   ○ 11
○ 6   ○ 16

Algebra: Missing Addends

Write the missing addend.

1. Jen has 7 pennies. She finds some more pennies. Now she has 12 pennies. How many pennies did Jen find?

$\underline{7} + \underline{5} = \underline{12}$

Jen found _5_ pennies.

2. Isha drew some pictures yesterday. Today she drew 8 more. Now she has 11 pictures. How many pictures did Isha draw yesterday?

$\underline{8} + \underline{} = \underline{11}$

Isha drew __ pictures yesterday.

3. Max saw 9 green fish and some red fish. He saw 14 fish in all. How many red fish did Max see?

$\underline{9} + \underline{} = \underline{14}$

Max saw ___ red fish.

4. Zach has 6 marbles. He finds some more marbles. Now he has 15 marbles. How many marbles did Zach find?

$\underline{6} + \underline{} = \underline{15}$

Zach found ___ marbles.

Mark the correct answer.

5. Elly has 7 big boxes and some small boxes. She has 10 boxes in all. How many small boxes does she have?

○ 3   ○ 7

○ 4   ○ 10

6. There are 13 cows in a field. There are 4 white cows. The rest are brown. How many brown cows are there?

○ 7   ○ 10

○ 9   ○ 13

Understand Plan Solve Check

Algebra: Names for Numbers

Solve.

---

1. Miko wrote a number name for 14. Her number name used addition. It used the number 7. What was Miko's number name for 14?

$$\underline{7} + \underline{7}$$

2. Alvin wrote a number name for 6. His number name used subtraction. It began with the number 10. What was Alvin's number name for 6?

$$\underline{} - \underline{}$$

---

3. Umi wrote a number name for 5. Her number name used subtraction. It began with the number 8. What was Umi's number name for 5?

$$\underline{} - \underline{}$$

4. Craig wrote a number name for 18. His number name used addition. It used the number 9. What was Craig's number name for 18?

$$\underline{} + \underline{}$$

---

5. Molly wrote a number name for 12. Her number name used addition. It used the number 7. What was Molly's number name for 12?

$$\underline{} + \underline{}$$

6. Raul wrote a number name for 7. His number name used subtraction. It began with the number 15. What was Raul's number name for 7?

$$\underline{} - \underline{}$$

Mark the correct answer.

7. Which is a number name for 9?

- ○ $3 + 5$
- ○ $11 - 2$
- ○ $6 + 4$
- ○ $15 - 0$

8. Which is a number name for 12?

- ○ $15 - 5$
- ○ $6 + 5$
- ○ $15 - 3$
- ○ $7 + 6$

Name _____

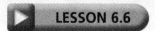

Understand   Plan   Solve   Check

Reading Strategy • Create Mental Images

Think about what is happening in the problem.
Then draw a picture or make a model.
Write the number sentence to solve.

1. Karla had 3 mice. Then she bought 6 more mice. How many mice did she have?

   __3__ ⊕ __6__ = __9__ mice

2. There were 10 cats in the yard. Then 4 of them went into the house. How many cats were still in the yard?

   ____ ○ ____ = ____ cats

3. Hal saw 6 birds in a tree and 5 birds on the ground. How many birds did Hal see?

   ____ ○ ____ = ____ birds

4. Jan has 7 goldfish. Ping has 3 goldfish. How many more goldfish does Jan have than Ping?

   ____ ○ ____ = ____ goldfish

Name _____

Mental Math: Add Tens

Solve.

1. Emma read 20 books. Dylan read 40. How many books did they read in all?

_____60_____ books

2. There are 30 children in Class 2A. There are 30 children in Class 2B. How many children are there in all?

_____ children

3. Elisha scored 10 points in Monday's game. She scored 20 points in Wednesday's game. How many points did she score in all?

_____ points

Mark the correct answer.

4. Which is another way to write 3 tens + 2 tens = 5 tens?

○ 20 + 20 = 40
○ 30 + 20 = 50
○ 30 + 40 = 70
○ 30 + 50 = 80

5. Which is another way to write 50 + 20 = 70?

○ 5 tens + 2 tens = 7 tens
○ 2 tens + 6 tens = 8 tens
○ 4 tens + 5 tens = 9 tens
○ 7 tens + 2 tens = 9 tens

Name _____

Mental Math: Count On Tens and Ones

Solve.
Count on to add.

1. There are 63 paper clips on the table. Ms. Kenner puts 20 more on the table. How many paper clips are there in all? _83_ paper clips	Say. Count on. _63_ _73_ , _83_ $63 + 20 = $ _83_
2. Nadine has 31 buttons. Her mother gives her 2 more. How many buttons does Nadine have in all? _____ buttons	Say. Count on. ____ ____ , ____ $31 + 2 = $ ____
3. Herbie has 54 shells. He buys 30 more. How many shells does he have in all? _____ shells	Say. Count on. ____ ____ , ____ , ____ $54 + 30 = $ ____

Mark the correct answer.

4. Which is the sum?
   $19 + 3 = $ _?_

   ○ 9
   ○ 11
   ○ 22
   ○ 27

5. Which is the sum?
   $49 + 10 = $ _?_

   ○ 39
   ○ 50
   ○ 59
   ○ 69

Understand Plan Solve Check

Regroup Ones as Tens

Use Workmat 3 and ⬚⬚⬚⬚⬚⬚⬚⬚⬚⬚ ⬚ .
Solve.

1. Ben and his father made 12 plain muffins and 8 raisin muffins. How many muffins did they make? _**20**_ muffins	2. It took 15 minutes to make lemonade. It took 7 minutes to clean up. How many minutes did it take in all? _____ minutes
3. Mrs. Lewis used 18 apples for applesauce. Then she used 6 apples to make more applesauce. How many apples did she use? _____ apples	4. The baker made 23 loaves of white bread and 6 loaves of wheat bread. How many loaves of bread did he make? _____ loaves of bread

Mark the correct answer.

5. Maria bought 13 bagels. Then she bought 8 more. How many bagels did she buy?

○ 5

○ 11

○ 15

○ 21

6. Tasha ate 11 grapes. Then she ate 5 more. How many grapes did Tasha eat?

○ 6

○ 12

○ 16

○ 26

Understand   Plan   Solve   Check

Model 2-Digit Addition

Use Workmat 3 and ⬜⬜⬜⬜⬜⬜⬜⬜⬜⬜ ⬜ .

Solve.

---

1. Paul sees 11 deer on Monday. He sees 16 deer on Tuesday. How many deer does he see on both days together?

_27_ deer

2. Carol sees 16 rabbits on Tuesday. She sees 21 rabbits on Wednesday. How many rabbits does she see on both days together?

_____ rabbits

---

3. John sees 15 newts on Wednesday. He sees 9 newts on Thursday. How many newts does he see in all?

_____ newts

4. Natalie sees 12 chipmunks on Thursday. She sees 19 chipmunks on Friday. How many chipmunks does she see on both days together?

_____ chipmunks

Mark the correct answer.

5. Jen sees 13 squirrels on Saturday and 18 squirrels on Sunday. How many squirrels does she see in all?

○ 21

○ 25

○ 31

○ 35

6. Jon sees 11 spiders on Monday and 12 spiders on Tuesday. How many spiders does he see in all?

○ 23

○ 24

○ 29

○ 32

Name _____

Understand   Plan   Solve   Check

Reading Strategy • Create Mental Images

Ray counts 12 robins and 9 sparrows.
How many birds does he count in all?

Picture the problem.

Choose a way to solve the problem.

Make a model ▢.
Draw a picture ✏️.
Write a number sentence ✏️.

Solve. $\underline{12} + \underline{9} = \underline{21}$

Ray counts $\underline{21}$ birds.

Picture the problems.
Then solve.

1. Tony has 16 peaches. Amber has 8 peaches. How many peaches do they have in all?

   _____ peaches

---

2. Loni ran 12 blocks on Monday. He ran 15 blocks on Tuesday. How many blocks did he run altogether?

   _____ blocks

Understand | Plan | Solve | Check

Add 1-Digit Numbers

Use Workmat 3 and ▭▭▭▭▭ ▯. Add.

1. Ian has 29 animal stickers. He has 5 flower stickers. How many stickers does he have in all?

__34__ stickers

2. There are 14 girls and 9 boys in Jani's class. How many children are in Jani's class altogether?

_____ children

3. Kata reads 33 pages of her book in the morning. She reads 6 more pages in the afternoon. How many pages does Kata read in all?

_____ pages

4. Dale makes a necklace with 48 small beads and 8 large beads. How many beads did Dale use to make the necklace?

_____ beads

5. Miko's garden has 56 yellow tulips and 7 red tulips. How many red and yellow tulips are in Miko's garden?

_____ tulips

6. The Rangers won the game against the Eagles. The score was 23 to 8. How many points did both teams score in all?

_____ points

Mark the correct answer.

7. Caleb has 58 stamps in his collection. His grandmother gives him 4 more stamps. How many stamps does Caleb have now?

○ 54   ○ 62
○ 60   ○ 68

8. Sara counts 23 robins in the tree. She counts 7 sparrows in the same tree. How many robins and sparrows did Sara count?

○ 16   ○ 33
○ 30   ○ 40

Name _____

Add 2-Digit Numbers

Use Workmat 3 and . Add.

1. Jen has 1 ten and 6 ones on her workmat. Then she puts down 2 more tens and 6 more ones. After she regroups, how many ones does Jen have?

___2___ ones

2. Ollie has 3 tens and 4 ones on his workmat. Then he puts down 1 more ten and 6 more ones. After he regroups, how many tens does Ollie have?

_____ tens

3. Yan rides her bicycle 14 blocks to her friend's house. Then she rides 16 blocks to her grandmother's house. How many blocks did Yan ride her bicycle in all?

_____ blocks

4. Will does 26 situps in the morning. He does 18 more situps in the evening. How many situps does Will do in all?

_____ situps

5. Ida has 24 CDs. Her sister has 36 CDs. How many CDs do Ida and her sister have together?

_____ CDs

6. Taylor puts 47 pennies in his piggy bank. He adds 28 more pennies. How many pennies are in Taylor's piggy bank now?

_____ pennies

Mark the correct answer.

7. Kyle has 54 marbles. He buys 16 more marbles. How many marbles does Kyle have now?

○ 60   ○ 70
○ 69   ○ 80

8. Debra reads for 36 minutes on Monday. She reads for 28 minutes on Tuesday. How many minutes does Debra read in all?

○ 54   ○ 74
○ 64   ○ 84

Understand   Plan   Solve   Check

More 2-Digit Addition

Add. Regroup if you need to.

1. The Mustangs baseball team won 17 games. They lost 14 games. How many games did the Mustangs play?

__31__ games

2. The store has 25 large baskets of fruit. It has 15 small baskets of fruit. How many baskets of fruit does the store have in all?

_____ baskets

3. Mark's dog weighs 47 pounds. His cat weighs 16 pounds. How many pounds do the dog and cat weigh together?

_____ pounds

4. Chris swims for 24 minutes. He rides his bike for 48 minutes. How many minutes does Mark swim and ride his bike?

_____ minutes

5. Rita reads 23 pages in her book in the morning. She reads 27 more pages before bed time. How many pages does she read in all?

_____ pages

6. There are 17 houses on one side of Elm Street. There are 16 houses on the other side. How many houses in all are on Elm Street?

_____ houses

Mark the correct answer.

7. The bus travels 34 miles. Then it travels 18 miles. How many miles does the bus travel in all?

○ 44   ○ 50
○ 46   ○ 52

8. Marco buys 2 bags of carrots. One bag has 17 carrots. The other bag has 24 carrots. How many carrots did Marco buy in all?

○ 31   ○ 41
○ 40   ○ 51

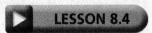

Practice 2-Digit Addition

	Girls	Boys
Grade 2	35	45
Grade 3	41	28

Use the chart to answer the questions.

1. How many children are in Grade 2?

__80__ children

2. How many boys are there in the two grades?

_____ boys

3. How many girls are there in the two grades?

_____ girls

4. How many children are in Grade 3?

_____ children

Mark the correct answer.

5. There are 26 girls and 29 boys in Grade 5. How many children are there in all?

○ 45
○ 55
○ 65

6. There are 36 boys and 40 girls in Grade 1. How many children are there in Grade 1?

○ 40
○ 64
○ 76

Rewrite 2-Digit Addition

Rewrite the numbers.
Solve.

1. There are 15 children on the bus.
   There are 21 adults on the bus. How
   many people are on the bus in all?

   $\underline{15} + \underline{21} = \underline{36}$ people

   $$\begin{array}{r} 1\,|\,5 \\ +\ 2\,|\,1 \\ \hline 3\,|\,6 \end{array}$$

2. Josh and Hanna made a tower with
   24 blocks. They added 37 more
   blocks. How many blocks did Josh
   and Hanna use in all?

   _____ + _____ = _____ blocks

   $+$ ___

3. Kendra took the elevator up 18 floors.
   Then she walked up 7 more floors.
   How many floors did Kendra go up?

   _____ + _____ = _____ floors

4. Last year the Panthers hit 58 home
   runs. This year they hit 34 home
   runs. How many home runs did they
   hit altogether?

   _____ + _____ = _____ home runs

Mark the correct answer.

5. 49 + 15 =

   ○ 54   ○ 63

   ○ 55   ○ 64

6. 37 + 16 =

   ○ 43   ○ 63

   ○ 53   ○ 65

Understand   Plan   Solve   Check

Estimate Sums

Use the number line to help you round.
Estimate the sum.

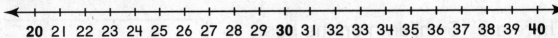

20 21 22 23 24 25 26 27 28 29 **30** 31 32 33 34 35 36 37 38 39 **40**

1. There are 22 roses on one bush.
   There are 31 roses on another bush.
   About how many roses are there
   in all?

   about __50__ roses

2. There are 39 ladybugs on the
   flowers. There are 23 ladybugs on
   the tree. About how many ladybugs
   are there in all?

   about _____ ladybugs

3. Pablo found 29 large shells at the
   beach. He found 24 small shells.
   About how many shells did Pablo
   find?

   about _____ shells

4. Tami sells 32 bags of peanuts. Her
   sister sells 38 bags. About how many
   bags of peanuts did they sell in all?

   about _____ bags of peanuts

Estimate the sum.
Mark the correct answer.

5. 39 + 39 =

   ○ 40   ○ 60
   ○ 50   ○ 80

6. 27 + 24 =

   ○ 50   ○ 80
   ○ 60   ○ 90

Name _____

Understand Plan Solve Check

Reading Strategy • Choose Important Words

Ray put <u>25 stickers</u> in one book.
He put <u>36 stickers</u> in another book.
How many stickers did Ray use <u>in all</u>?

Underline the words that help you solve the problem.

Then solve. 36 + 25 = 61 stickers

_____

Underline the words that help you solve
the problem. Then solve.

1. Haley saw 32 birds this week. She saw 41 birds last week. How many birds did Haley see in all? _____ birds	
2. Fred sees 28 trucks on the highway. He also sees 16 vans. How many trucks and vans does Fred see altogether? _____ trucks and vans	
3. Ella buys two bags of apples. One bag has 12 apples. The other bag has 18 apples. How many apples did Ella buy in all? _____ apples	

Name _____

Understand Plan Solve Check

Mental Math: Subtract Tens

There are 10 trading cards in 1 pack.
Write a subtraction sentence for each problem.

1. Mara has 7 packs of trading cards. She gives Greg 2 of them. How many trading cards does Mara have left?

   _7_ tens − _2_ tens = _5_ tens

2. Leon has 8 packs of trading cards. Evan borrows 5 packs. How many trading cards does Leon have left?

   _80_ − _50_ = _30_

3. Trudy has 3 packs of trading cards. She gives Philip 1 pack. How many trading cards does Trudy have left?

   ____ − ____ = ____

4. Michael has 5 packs of trading cards. Will borrows 4 packs. How many trading cards does Michael have left?

   ___ tens − ___ tens = ___ ten

Mark the correct answer.

5. Which is the difference?
   9 tens − 7 tens = _?_

   ○ 2 tens
   ○ 3 tens
   ○ 4 tens
   ○ 8 tens

6. Which is the difference?
   60 − 10 = _?_

   ○ 70
   ○ 50
   ○ 30
   ○ 20

Name _____

Understand Plan Solve Check

Mental Math: Count Back Tens and Ones

Write the subtraction sentence. Count back to solve.

1. Matteo made a tower with 62 blocks. His brother took 3 blocks from the top. How many blocks are part of the tower now?

____ – ____ = ____ blocks

2. Reese played 17 games of tic-tac-toe. She lost only 2 of them. How many games did she win?

____ – ____ = ____ games

3. Gavin had 87 trading cards. He gave 20 of them away. How many trading cards did he have left?

____ – ____ = ____ trading cards

4. Ella picked 46 flowers. She gave 10 of them to her grandmother. How many flowers did Ella keep?

____ – ____ = ____ flowers

5. Hoy bought 20 balloons. On his way to the party, 3 of them popped. How many balloons did he have left?

____ – ____ = ____ balloons

6. A farmer brought 64 baskets of tomatoes to the market. He sold 30 of them. How many baskets of tomatoes were left?

____ – ____ = ____ baskets

Mark the correct answer.

7. Tyra brought 54 marbles to her friend's house. She left 3 of them there. How many marbles did she bring home?

○ 3   ○ 51

○ 50   ○ 57

8. Kai bought 25 yo-yos for his party. He gave away 20 to his friends. How many were left?

○ 5   ○ 20

○ 15   ○ 25

Name _____

Regroup Tens as Ones

Use Workmat 3 and   .
Subtract. Write how many tens and ones are left.

1. There are 17 people sledding. Then 9 people go home. How many are left?

__8__ people

__0__ tens __8__ ones

2. There are 23 people sledding. There are 5 people skating. How many more people are sledding than skating?

____ more people

____ ten ____ ones

3. There are 22 boys skating. There are 7 girls skating. How many more boys than girls are skating?

____ more boys

____ ten ____ ones

4. There are 30 people making snow forts. Then 8 go home. How many people are left?

____ people

____ tens ____ ones

Mark the correct answer.

5. There are 38 children at the game. Then 6 go home. How many children are left?

○ 22 ○ 32

○ 26 ○ 44

6. There are 24 red balloons. There are 8 blue balloons. How many more red than blue balloons are there?

○ 32 ○ 22

○ 26 ○ 16

Name _____

LESSON 9.4

Understand Plan Solve Check

Model 2-Digit Subtraction

Use Workmat 3 and ▭▭▭▭▭ ▭.
Subtract.

1. There are 24 children in a play. 11 children dance. The other children sing. How many children sing?

_13_ children

2. There are 30 chairs at the play. There are 13 couches. How many more chairs than couches are there?

_____ more chairs

3. Hannah sold 21 tickets for the play. Anna sold 15 tickets. How many more tickets did Hannah sell than Anna?

_____ more tickets

4. On Friday, 44 people came to the play. On Saturday, 25 fewer people came. How many came on Saturday?

_____ people

Mark the correct answer.

5. There are 25 girls and 16 boys in the play. How many more girls than boys are in the play?

○ 9
○ 14
○ 26
○ 34

6. Yolanda sold 39 adult tickets and 18 student tickets. How many more adult tickets than student tickets did she sell?

○ 11
○ 18
○ 21
○ 26

Name _____

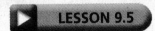

Understand   Plan   Solve   Check

Reading Strategy • Choose Important Words

Important words can help you understand a problem.

Aram has 20 **stamps**.
He uses 4 of them.
How many stamps are **left**?

What is the problem about? _____ stamps _____

What are you asked to find? ___ How many stamps are left? ___

Will you add or subtract? _____ subtract _____

Solve the problem. 20 − 4 = ___16___

Aram has __16__ stamps left.

Solve. Underline important words.
Use workmat 3 and ▭▭▭▭ ▯.

1. Cora has 17 games at her house. She has 8 games at her grandmother's house. How many games does Cora have in all?

___ ◯ ___ ◯ ___
games

2. Jody and his friends play with 24 toy trucks. They lose 5 of them in the sand box. How many toy trucks are left?

___ ◯ ___ ◯ ___
toy trucks

3. There are 18 books on the shelf. People take 5 of the books to read. How many books are left?

___ ◯ ___ ◯ ___
books

4. There are 12 people in the swimming pool. Then 10 more people jump in. How many people are in the pool now?

___ ◯ ___ ◯ ___
people

Understand Plan Solve Check

Subtract 1-Digit Numbers

Use Workmat 3 and ⬜⬜⬜⬜⬜⬜⬜⬜ ⬜. Subtract.

1. Terry finds 17 shells. Amy finds 9 shells. How many more shells does Terry find?

_____ shells

2. There are 22 families on the beach. Then 8 families go home. How many families are left?

_____ families

3. There are 24 children swimming. 6 other children are making a sand castle. How many more children are swimming?

_____ children

4. Terry finds 14 shells before lunch. He finds 7 shells after lunch. How many more shells does he find before lunch?

_____ shells

5. Mark counts 32 fish. Maria counts 9 fish. How many more fish does Mark count?

_____ fish

6. Jean has 23 shells. She gives 5 shells to Tony. How many shells does Jean still have?

_____ shells

Mark the correct answer.

7.

tens	ones
☐	☐
4	2
−	7

○ 33
○ 35
○ 37
○ 40

8.

tens	ones
☐	☐
6	7
−	8

○ 49
○ 59
○ 61
○ 63

Name _____

Subtract 2-Digit Numbers

Use Workmat 3 and ⬜⬜⬜⬜⬜⬜ ⬜.
Solve.

1. On Saturday morning 32 cars and 15 vans came to the car wash. How many more cars than vans came? ____17____ more cars	$$\begin{array}{r} \overset{2\ \ 12}{\cancel{3}\cancel{2}} \\ -\ 1\ 5 \\ \hline 1\ 7 \end{array}$$
2. One day 33 cars and 17 trucks are washed. How many more cars than trucks are washed? _____ cars	
3. 32 cars were washed in the morning. 27 were washed in the afternoon. How many more cars were washed in the morning? _____ cars	

Mark the correct answer.

4.

tens	ones
☐	☐
4	5
− 1	9

◯ 36
◯ 34
◯ 26
◯ 24

5.

tens	ones
☐	☐
5	3
− 2	6

◯ 17
◯ 27
◯ 39
◯ 43

Understand   Plan   Solve   Check

More 2-Digit Subtraction

Solve.

1. Megan had 73 books at the garage sale. She sold 42. How many are left? __31__ books	$$\begin{array}{r} 73 \\ -42 \\ \hline 31 \end{array}$$
2. Cal has 24 toys for sale. He sells 16. How many are left? _____ toys	
3. There were 24 garden tools for sale. Brenda bought 10. How many were left? _____ garden tools	

Mark the correct answer.

4.

tens	ones
☐	☐
3	2
− 1	6

○ 14
○ 16
○ 24
○ 26

5.

tens	ones
☐	☐
4	3
− 2	5

○ 13
○ 16
○ 18
○ 28

Rewrite 2-Digit Subtraction

Solve. Show your work.

1. There are 65 students on the playground. 47 are wearing sneakers. How many are not wearing sneakers?

   $$
   \begin{array}{r}
   \overset{5}{6}\,\overset{15}{5} \\
   -\ 4\ 7 \\
   \hline
   1\ 8
   \end{array}
   $$

   _18_ students

2. There are 83 students eating lunch. 55 are eating hot lunches. How many students are not eating hot lunches?

   _____ students

3. There are 50 students in the library at Martin Luther King, Jr. Elementary School. 27 of them are girls. How many are boys?

   _____ boys

Mark the correct answer.

4. There are 30 teachers at City Elementary School. 14 of them are not wearing green today. How many of them are wearing green?

   ○ 24
   ○ 26
   ○ 16
   ○ 44

Estimate Differences

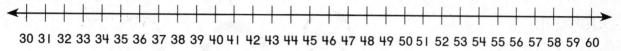

30 31 32 33 34 35 36 37 38 39 40 41 42 43 44 45 46 47 48 49 50 51 52 53 54 55 56 57 58 59 60

Use the number line to round each number
to the nearest ten. Estimate the difference.

1. Morgan put 31 red beads and 42 blue beads on a string. About how many more blue beads did she use? about _____ blue beads	
2. Sherry chose 58 shells and 42 beads to make a necklace. About how many more shells did she choose? about _____ shells	
3. John needs 55 beads to make a key chain. He has 33 beads. About how many more beads does John need? about _____ beads	

Estimate the difference. Mark the correct answer

4. Bria's necklace has 57 white beads and 38 black beads. About how many more white beads are on the necklace?

   ○ 10   ○ 30

   ○ 20   ○ 40

5. 45 beads fell on the floor. Clay picked up 35 of them. About how many more beads are still on the floor?

   ○ 10   ○ 30

   ○ 20   ○ 40

Name _____

Understand · Plan · Solve · Check

Algebra: Use Addition to Check Subtraction

Subtract.
Add to check.

1. Devin cut out 74 snowflakes and 38 stars. How many more snowflakes than stars did he cut out? _36_ more snowflakes	$\begin{array}{r} \overset{6}{\cancel{7}}\overset{14}{\cancel{4}} \\ -\ 38 \\ \hline 36 \end{array}$ $\begin{array}{r} \overset{1}{3}6 \\ +\ 38 \\ \hline 74 \end{array}$
2. Zach made 61 moons. Jan made 9 moons. How many more moons did Zach make? _____ more moons	
3. Lana wants 84 stars. She has made 37. How many more stars must she make? _____ more stars	

Mark the correct answer.

4. Which numbers should you add to check the subtraction problem?

$$\begin{array}{r} 57 \\ -\ 25 \\ \hline 32 \end{array}$$

○ $\begin{array}{r} 32 \\ +\ 25 \end{array}$ ○ $\begin{array}{r} 57 \\ +\ 25 \end{array}$

○ $\begin{array}{r} 32 \\ +\ 57 \end{array}$ ○ $\begin{array}{r} 32 \\ +\ 32 \end{array}$

Name _____

Understand Plan Solve Check

Reading Strategy: Words That Compare

Words that compare can help you solve problems.

Ben, Tani, and Mira are fast runners. At the track meet, Mira ran <u>slower</u> than Ben. Tani ran <u>fastest</u> of all. What place did each runner get?

1. Look for words that compare, such as *slower* and *fastest*. Underline the words.

2. Sentences that compare give you clues. Use each clue to place the runners in order.

   Tani ran fastest of all. is a good clue. What place did Tani get?

   ___first___ place

3. Solve the problem. Write who won each place.

FIRST PLACE — Tani   SECOND PLACE — Ben   THIRD PLACE — Mira

   Look for words that compare. Then solve.

4. Ray, Alex, and Jesse each built a sand castle. Jesse built the shortest castle. Ray's castle was shorter than Alex's, but taller than Jesse's. What is the order of the castles from tallest to shortest?

_____   _____   _____

tallest ◄———————————————► shortest

Name _____

Different Ways to Add

Solve.

1. There were 17 people on one train. There were 30 people on another train. How many people were on both trains?

   _____ people

2. Ramon bought a box of 24 pencils. His friend gave him 3 more pencils. How many pencils did Ramon have in all?

   _____ pencils

3. Ms. Grant's class has 18 boys and 17 girls. How many children are in the class?

   _____ children

4. There are 43 ducks and 30 geese at the pond. How many ducks and geese are at the pond in all?

   _____ ducks and geese

5. Juan is making a bookcase. He needs 26 long nails and 26 short nails. How many nails does he need in all?

   _____ nails

6. Mr. Hoi collects CDs of jazz music and rock music. He has 35 jazz CDs and 27 rock CDs. How many CDs does he have?

   _____ CDs

Mark the correct answer.

7. $32 + 30 =$
   ○ 42
   ○ 52
   ○ 62
   ○ 72

8. $48 + 27 =$
   ○ 64
   ○ 65
   ○ 74
   ○ 75

Practice 2-Digit Addition

Marlee, Doug, Hector, and Troy are in a swim club. The chart shows the number of laps each person swam last week. Use the chart to solve the problems.

Swimmer	Number of Laps
Marlee	35
Doug	14
Hector	46
Troy	19

1. How many laps did Marlee swim? How many laps did Doug swim? How many laps did they swim in all?

   Marlee: _____ laps

   Doug: _____ laps

   _____ laps in all

2. How many laps did Hector swim? How many laps did Troy swim? How many laps did they swim in all?

   Hector: _____ laps

   Troy: _____ laps

   _____ laps in all

3. How many laps did Marlee and Hector swim in all?

   _____ laps

4. How many laps did Troy and Doug swim in all?

   _____ laps

5. How many laps did Marlee and Troy swim in all?

   _____ laps

6. How many laps did Hector and Doug swim in all?

   _____ laps

Mark the correct answer.

7. Raul ran for 15 minutes. He biked for another 26 minutes. How many minutes did he spend running and biking?

   ◯ 21   ◯ 40
   ◯ 31   ◯ 41

8. Nora made 23 saves in a soccer game. She made 19 saves in the next game. How many saves did she make in all?

   ◯ 40   ◯ 42
   ◯ 41   ◯ 43

Name _____

Column Addition

Solve.

1. A street runs for three blocks. There are 14 houses on the first block. There are 18 houses on the second block. There are 24 houses on the third block. How many houses are on the street? _56_ houses	$\begin{array}{r} 14 \\ 18 \\ +24 \\ \hline 56 \end{array}$
2. It takes Liat 15 minutes to eat breakfast, 25 minutes to eat lunch, and 35 minutes to eat dinner. How many minutes does it take him to eat all three meals? _____ minutes	
3. A bookcase has 3 shelves. The top shelf has 8 books, the middle shelf has 29 books, and the bottom shelf has 31 books. How many books are in the bookcase? _____ books	
4. Three friends knit scarves. Each scarf is 15 inches long. What is the total length of the scarves? _____ inches	

Add. Mark the correct answer.

5. $25 + 17 + 44 =$ _____

   ○ 74   ○ 84

   ○ 76   ○ 86

6. $14 + 19 + 29 =$ _____

   ○ 52   ○ 72

   ○ 62   ○ 82

Name _____

Different Ways to Subtract

Subtract using different ways.

1. Nat had 75 trading cards. He gave 3 away. How many trading cards does he have left?

_____ trading cards

2. There were 27 birds in the tree. Then 18 flew away. How many birds were still in the tree?

_____ birds

3. Karen has 34 bows. She gives 3 of them away. How many bows does she have left?

_____ bows

4. There are 47 fish in the pond. There are 58 fish in the lake. How many more fish are in the lake?

_____ fish

5. Valerie's basketball team scored 57 points. The other team scored 30 points. How many more points did Valerie's team score?

_____ points

6. Lisa has 52 pennies in a box. She takes 18 of the pennies out and uses them to play a game. How many pennies are left in the box?

_____ pennies

Mark the correct answer.

7. $55 - 10 =$
○ 35
○ 45
○ 50
○ 55

8. $61 - 28 =$
○ 33
○ 34
○ 43
○ 48

Name _____

Practice 2-Digit Subtraction

Complete the subtraction sentence. Solve.

1. There are 47 chickens in the barn. 23 of them lay eggs. How many chickens do not lay eggs?

$\underline{47} - \underline{23} = \underline{24}$

$\underline{24}$ chickens

2. There are 22 sheep on the farm. 18 sheep are in the barn. How many sheep are not in the barn?

_____ − _____ = _____

_____ sheep

3. There are 56 cows in the barn. 20 cows give milk. How many cows do not give milk?

_____ − _____ = _____

_____ cows

4. There are 38 horses in the pasture. 15 are brown. How many horses are not brown?

_____ − _____ = _____

_____ horses

5. There are 26 pigs in the pen. 11 pigs have spots. How many pigs do not have spots?

_____ − _____ = _____

_____ pigs

6. There are 46 goats in the field. 26 are eating hay. How many goats are not eating hay?

_____ − _____ = _____

_____ goats

Mark the correct answer.

7. What is the difference for 93 − 52?

○ 40   ○ 48

○ 41   ○ 51

8. What is the difference for 93 − 39?

○ 64   ○ 54

○ 60   ○ 52

Mixed Practice

The chart shows the number of games each team won. Use the chart to solve the problems.

Team	Games Won
Bluebirds	24
Hawks	17
Robins	36
Crows	9

1. How many games did the Hawks and the Bluebirds win in all?

   _____ games

2. How many more games did the Hawks win than the Crows?

   _____ games

3. How many games did the Crows and the Robins win in all?

   _____ games

4. How many more games did the Robins win than the Crows?

   _____ games

5. How many games did the Bluebirds and the Robins win in all?

   _____ games

6. How many more games did the Bluebirds win than the Hawks?

   _____ games

Mark the correct answer.

7. $28 + 16 =$
   - ○ 32
   - ○ 34
   - ○ 42
   - ○ 44

8. $63 - 18 =$
   - ○ 44
   - ○ 45
   - ○ 54
   - ○ 55

Name _____

Understand Plan Solve Check

Reading Strategy: Sequence Events

Knowing the order in which things happen
can help you solve math problems.

Greta had some buttons. First she gave
15 buttons to her sister. Then she gave 10
buttons to her brother. Now Greta has 28 buttons.
How many buttons did she have to start?

1. First Greta gave ___15___ buttons to her sister.

2. Then she gave ___10___ buttons to her brother.

3. Now Greta has ___28___ buttons.

4. Solve by working backward.

   28 buttons now   38 total buttons
  + 10 buttons to her brother + 15 buttons to her sister
   38 total buttons   53 total buttons

Greta had ___53___ buttons at the start.

Think about the order in which things happen. Then solve.

5. Ilana had a bag of stickers.
   She gave 20 stickers to Fan
   and 8 stickers to Lou. That
   left 21 stickers in the bag.
   How many stickers were
   in the bag to start?

   _____ stickers

6. Harley collected some rocks
   in the morning. He collected
   42 more rocks in the
   afternoon. He collected
   71 rocks in all. How many
   rocks did he collect in the
   morning?

   _____ rocks

Name _____

Understand Plan Solve Check

Pennies, Nickels, and Dimes

Count on to find the total amount.
Write the name of the toy that costs the same amount.

24¢ bear   18¢ lion   37¢ frog   30¢ mouse

1.

<u>bear</u>

2.

_____

3.

_____

Mark the correct answer.

4. Which is the total amount?

○ 7¢   ○ 8¢
○ 12¢   ○ 13¢

5. Which is the total amount?

○ 7¢   ○ 12¢
○ 17¢   ○ 22¢

Name _____

Quarters and Half-Dollars

Draw coins to solve.

1. Wayne has 1 half-dollar, 3 nickels, and 2 pennies.
How much money does he have?

67 ¢

2. Amy has 1 quarter and 4 nickels.
How much money does she have?

_____ ¢

3. Leon has 1 half-dollar, 1 quarter, and 4 pennies.
How much money does he have?

_____ ¢

Mark the correct answer.

4. Which is the total amount?

- ○ 95¢
- ○ 90¢
- ○ 85¢
- ○ not here

5. Which is the total amount?

- ○ 71¢
- ○ 66¢
- ○ 61¢
- ○ not here

Name _____

Count Collections

Think of a way to solve each problem.

1. Mei had these coins.

She spent 1 quarter. How much money did she have left? __21__¢

2. These coins are in Roger's bank.

Roger adds 1 nickel. How much money
is in Roger's bank now?   _____¢

3. Dorothy has these coins.

She gets another coin. Now she has 50¢.
What coin did she get?   _____

Mark the correct answer.

4. Which is the total amount?

○ 36¢   ○ 41¢

○ 46¢   ○ 51¢

5. Which is the total amount?

○ 20¢   ○ 17¢

○ 22¢   ○ 16¢

Understand Plan Solve Check

1 Dollar

Draw and label coins to solve.

1. Bruce has 11 coins that equal $1.00. Some are dimes. Some are nickels. How many of each coin does he have?

    __9__ dimes   __2__ nickels

2. Antonio has 11 coins that equal $1.00. Some are half-dollars. Some are nickels. How many of each coin does Antonio have?

    _____ half-dollar   _____ nickels

3. Neil has 8 coins that equal $1.00. Some are quarters. Some are nickels. How many of each coin does Neil have?

    _____ quarters   _____ nickels

Mark the correct answer.

4. How many equal $1.00?

    ○ 2   ○ 10
    ○ 4   ○ 25

5. How many equal $1.00?

    ○ 2   ○ 10
    ○ 4   ○ 20

Add Money

Solve.

1. Gil buys a carrot for 25¢. He buys a tomato for 55¢. How much money does he spend altogether?

_____

2. Kareem has 22¢ in one pocket. He has 49¢ in another pocket. How much money does he have in all?

_____

3. Vijay's family has a yard sale. He sells one toy car for 38¢ and another for a nickel. How much money does he get in all?

_____

4. Kristin finds 9¢ one morning. She finds 37¢ two days later. How much money does she find in all?

_____

5. Ms. Bowers buys a newspaper and a postcard. The newspaper costs 35¢. The postcard costs a quarter. How much money does she spend in all?

_____

6. Serena has 48¢ in her piggy bank. She add 2 quarters to the bank. How much money does she have in her bank now?

_____

Mark the correct answer.

7. 45¢ + 38¢

　○ 73¢　　　○ 85¢

　○ 83¢　　　○ 93¢

8. 27¢ + 14¢

　○ 31¢　　　○ 41¢

　○ 32¢　　　○ 42¢

Name _____

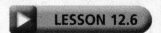

Reading Strategy • Use Graphic Aids

Jack has 8 coins. They are dimes and nickels.
He has more dimes than nickels. What
coins could Jack have?

You can use a chart to solve the problem.

Dimes	Nickels	Total
7	1	75¢
6	2	70¢
5	3	65¢

1. Which combination of coins
   has the greatest value?   _____ dimes _____ nickel

2. Which combination of coins
   has the least value?   _____ dimes _____ nickels

---

3. Tanya has 7 coins. She has only
   quarters and pennies. She has more pennies
   than quarters. What coins could Tanya have?

Quarters	Pennies	Total

4. Which combination of coins
   has the greatest value?   _____ quarters _____ pennies

5. Which combination of coins
   has the least value?   _____ quarter   _____ pennies

Make the Same Amounts

Draw and label the coins.
Write the amount.

1. Greg has 15¢. His father gives him 30¢. How much money does Greg have now? ___45___ ¢	
2. Judy has 40¢. She earns 50¢ raking leaves. How much money does she have now? _____ ¢	
3. Bob has 1 quarter, 2 dimes, and 4 pennies. How much money does he have? _____ ¢	

Mark the correct answer.

4. Which is the total amount?

- ○ 55¢
- ○ 40¢
- ○ 35¢
- ○ 31¢

Name _____

Understand Plan Solve Check

Algebra: Same Amounts Using the Fewest Coins

Solve. Then draw coins to show the same amount
with the fewest coins. Label each coin.

I. Allen has I quarter, I nickel,
and 5 pennies. How much
money does he have?

_**35**_ ¢

2. Paul has 4 dimes and 2 nickels.
How much money does he
have?

_____ ¢

Mark the correct answer.

3. Which is the total amount?

○ 50¢
○ 35¢
○ 30¢
○ 26¢

4. Which is the total amount?

○ 40¢
○ 45¢
○ 46¢
○ 55¢

Name _____

Understand Plan Solve Check

Compare Amounts

Solve.

1. Mara has 1 quarter, 1 dime, and 1 nickel. Joe has 3 dimes and 1 nickel. Who has the greater amount?

   _____

   _ _ _ _ _ _ _ _ _ _ _ _ _ _

   _____

2. Elroy has 1 half dollar and 2 dimes. Toby has 1 quarter, 3 dimes, and 2 nickels. Who has the lesser amount?

   _____

   _ _ _ _ _ _ _ _ _ _ _ _ _ _

   _____

3. Kisha has 3 dimes, 2 nickels, and 5 pennies. Lucy has 1 quarter and 4 nickels. Do they have the same amount or different amounts?

   _____

   _ _ _ _ _ _ _ _ _ _ _ _ _ _

   _____

4. Flo has 1 quarter, 2 dimes, and 1 nickel. Luis has 1 half dollar and 3 nickels. Do they have the same amount or different amounts?

   _____

   _ _ _ _ _ _ _ _ _ _ _ _ _ _

   _____

5. Taro has 2 dimes, 4 nickels, and 3 pennies. Ben has 1 quarter, 1 nickel, and 4 pennies. Who has the greater amount?

   _____

   _ _ _ _ _ _ _ _ _ _ _ _ _ _

   _____

6. Kari has 2 quarters, 1 dime, and 1 nickel. Mary has 1 quarter, 3 dimes, and 1 nickel. Who has the lesser amount?

   _____

   _ _ _ _ _ _ _ _ _ _ _ _ _ _

   _____

Mark your answer.

7. Which of the following is equal to 35¢?

   ○ 1 quarter, 1 dime

   ○ 2 dimes, 1 nickel

   ○ 5 nickels

   ○ 1 dime, 4 nickels

8. Which of the following is less than 20¢.

   ○ 2 dimes

   ○ 1 dime, 1 nickel

   ○ 5 nickels

   ○ 1 dime, 4 nickels

Name _____

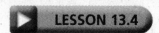

Compare Amounts to Prices

Write the names and prices of
toys the child might buy.

55¢   turtle   85¢   duck   45¢   cat   70¢   dog   95¢   fish

1. Sally has 65¢.

_____ cat ___ 45 ¢

_____ turtle ___ 55 ¢

2. Alex has 95¢.

_____ ¢

_____ ¢

3. Terry has 80¢.

_____ ¢

_____ ¢

4. James has 75¢.

_____ ¢

_____ ¢

Mark the correct answer.

5. Brad has

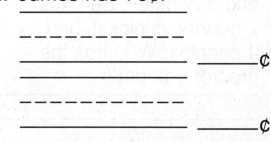

Does he have enough to
buy a toy that costs 60¢?

○ yes   ○ no

Name _____

Understand **Plan** **Solve** **Check**

Make Change to $1.00

Use coins to solve.

1. Jake has 40¢. He buys apple juice for 37¢. How much change does he get?

_____3_____ ¢

2. Kelly has 81¢. She buys a muffin for 79¢. How much change does she get?

_____ ¢

3. Kay has 2 quarters, 2 nickels, and 6 pennies. Does she have enough money to buy a pen for 65¢?

Yes   No

4. Gino has 1 half-dollar, 1 quarter, 1 dime, and 1 nickel. How much money does he have?

_____ ¢

5. Les has 3 quarters, 1 dime, and 4 pennies. How much money does he have?

_____ ¢

6. Julie has 3 dimes, 4 nickels, and 5 pennies. How much money does she have?

_____ ¢

Mark the correct answer.

7. You have 46¢. You buy a toy car for 42¢. Your change is _____.

○ 2¢
○ 3¢
○ 4¢
○ 5¢

8. You have 72¢. You buy a ball for 69¢. Your change is _____.

○ 2¢
○ 3¢
○ 4¢
○ 5¢

Name _____

Understand   Plan   Solve   Check

Subtract Money

Solve.

1. Allie buys a toy for 72¢. She has 95¢. How much change does she get?

    _____¢

2. Steve has 47¢. Juan has 64¢. How much more money does Juan have?

    _____¢

3. Malik has 35¢. He wants to buy a book for 87¢. How much more money does he need?

    _____¢

4. Tara has saved 46¢. Maya has saved 39¢. How much money do they have altogether?

    _____¢

5. Chelsea has 50¢. She buys a gift for 42¢. How much money does Chelsea have left?

    _____¢

6. Mike has 22¢. Paul has 32¢ more than Mike. How much money does Paul have?

    _____¢

Mark the correct answer.

7. Roberto has 75¢. He buys a ball for 59¢. How much change does he get?

    ○ 16¢
    ○ 18¢
    ○ 25¢
    ○ 26¢

8. Diane has 37¢. Marie has 26¢. How much money do they have altogether?

    ○ 11¢
    ○ 21¢
    ○ 53¢
    ○ 63¢

Reading Strategy • Make Predictions

Sometimes a problem will ask you to
tell if something can happen.

Mark has 85¢. He wants to buy a
book about cars for 32¢. He wants
to buy a book about cats for 47¢.
Will Mark have enough money?

Estimate how much money Mark needs.   30¢ + 50¢ = 80¢

Will Mark have enough money?   Yes, 80¢ < 85¢

Check your estimate. 32¢ + 47¢ = 79¢   79¢ < 85¢

Solve. Make an estimate.
Then circle yes or no.

1. John has 45¢. He wants to
   buy an apple for 16¢. He
   wants to buy an orange for
   22¢. Will John have enough
   money?

   estimate: _____¢

   yes   no

2. Rosa has 85¢. She wants
   to buy a ball for 43¢. She
   wants to buy a doll for 52¢.
   Will Rosa have enough
   money?

   estimate: _____¢

   yes   no

3. Nancy sees a toy car that
   costs 19¢. She sees a toy
   boat that costs 33¢. Nancy
   has 65¢. Will she have
   enough money to buy
   the toys?

   estimate: _____¢

   yes   no

4. Lahn wants a marker
   for 27¢. He wants some
   stickers for 39¢. Lahn has
   60¢. Will he have enough
   money to buy the marker
   and stickers?

   estimate: _____¢

   yes   no

Name _____

Understand Plan Solve Check

Explore 1 Minute

Solve.

1. Jo is going to weed her garden. Will it take her more than or less than 1 minute?

    __more than__ 1 minute

2. Kinja throws the ball into the basket. Does it take him more than or less than 1 minute?

    _____ 1 minute

3. Shana goes to a concert. Will the concert last more than or less than 1 minute?

    _____ 1 minute

4. Yoshi is going to write a letter to his grandmother. Will it take him more than or less than 1 minute?

    _____ 1 minute

5. Darnell can make 2 paper airplanes in 1 minute. How many paper airplanes can he make in 5 minutes?

    _____ paper airplanes

6. It takes 3 minutes for Dawn to walk around the playground. How many minutes will it take her to walk around the playground 2 times?

    _____ minutes

Solve.
Mark the correct answer.

7. Which takes less than 1 minute?

    ○ pour a glass of water

    ○ watch a movie

    ○ read a book

8. Which takes more than 1 minute?

    ○ wave to a friend

    ○ snap your fingers

    ○ eat lunch

Time to the Hour

Solve.

1. Billy practices soccer for one hour each day. If he starts at 3:00, what time will practice end?

__4:00__

2. Tim leaves for school at 8:00 in the morning. He gets up one hour earlier. What time does Tim get up?

_____ o'clock

3. Rachel is watching a TV program. It started at 7:00. It will last for 1 hour. When will the program end?

____:____

4. It takes 1 hour for Laura to get to her grandmother's house. She leaves at 10 o'clock in the morning. What time will she get there?

_____ o'clock

5. Kevin finished his homework at 5:00. He started one hour earlier. What time did Kevin start to do his homework?

____:____

6. Lizzie went on a hike with friends. They left at 7:00 in the morning. They hiked for 2 hours. What time did the hike end?

_____ o'clock

Mark the correct answer.

7. Tony went to the park. He got there at 11:00 and stayed 1 hour. What time did he leave the park?

○ 10 o'clock

○ 11 o'clock

○ 12 o'clock

○ 1 o'clock

8. Sue was at the library for 1 hour. She left the library at 11 o'clock. What time did she get to the library?

○ 9:00 o'clock

○ 10:00 o'clock

○ 11:00 o'clock

○ 12:00 o'clock

Name _____

Understand   Plan   Solve   Check

Time to the Half-Hour

Solve.

1. May ate a peach at half past 6. What time was it when she ate the peach?

6:30

2. The baseball game starts at 30 minutes after 1. What time does the baseball game start?

_____

3. Reya will stop reading her book at 30 minutes before 4. When will she stop reading her book?

_____

4. The Fowler family will leave for the park at five thirty. When will they leave for the park?

_____

5. Kenji starts watching a movie at 30 minutes before 1. What time is it when he starts watching the movie?

_____

6. Andy's art class starts at half past 10. What time was it when the class started?

_____

Solve.
Mark the best answer.

7. What is another name for 3:30?

○ 30 minutes before 3
○ half past 3
○ 30 minutes after 4
○ none of these

8. What is another name for 10:30?

○ 30 minutes after 9
○ 30 minutes before 10
○ half past 11
○ none of these

PS78 **Problem Solving**

Name _____

Understand Plan Solve Check

Time to 15 Minutes

Solve.

1. Eric gets to the pool at
11:00 and starts swimming.
He swims for 30 minutes.
What time is it when
he stops swimming?

11:30

2. Mary starts reading her
book at 8 o'clock. She
stops reading 45 minutes
later. What time is it when
she stops reading?

_____:_____

3. Terry took his dog for a
walk at 4:00. They walked
for 15 minutes. What time
was it when they finished
walking?

_____:_____

4. It takes Harry 15 minutes
to get ready for school. If
he starts at 7 o'clock, what
time will he be ready?

_____:_____

5. Mark looked at the clock.
The hour hand pointed a
little past the 8. The minute
hand pointed to 3. What time
was it?

_____:_____

6. Andy looked at his watch.
The hour hand pointed
halfway between the 2 and
3. The minute hand pointed
to 6. What time was it?

_____:_____

Solve.
Mark the best answer.

7. What time comes before
8:15?

○ 8:00   ○ 8:30

○ 8:45   ○ 9:00

8. What time comes after
10:30?

○ 9:45   ○ 10:00

○ 10:15   ○ 10:45

Name _____

Understand Plan Solve Check

Minutes

Solve.

1. Grady feeds his cat when the clock says 4:42. Draw the minute hand on the clock to show the time.

2. Alan calls his friend when the clock says 2:25. Draw the minute hand on the clock to show the time.

3. Tracy turns on the radio at 7:16. Draw the minute hand on the clock to show the time.

4. At 10:08 LaToya goes out to weed the garden. Draw the minute hand on the clock to show the time.

Mark the correct answer.

5.

○ 2:42
○ 3:28
○ 3:42
○ 3:52

6.

○ 9:17
○ 10:12
○ 10:15
○ 10:17

(Understand) (Plan) (Solve) (Check)

Reading Strategy • Use Picture Clues

Using picture clues can help you solve problems.

Read the problem. Use the pictures to help you solve it.

Mr. Kim Leaves

Mr. Kim Gets Home

1. Mr. Kim goes to the supermarket at __10:00__.

2. He gets home at __10:35__.

3. How many minutes have passed? __35__ minutes

Look for picture clues. Solve the problems.

Fran Leaves

Fran Gets Back

4. Fran goes for a walk.

   She leaves at _____.

   She comes back at _____.

   How many minutes have passed? _____ minutes

---

5. Barry starts playing soccer at _____.

   He stops playing at _____.

   How much time has passed?

   _____ hours

Barry Starts Playing

Barry Stops Playing

Name _____

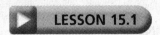

Understand Plan Solve Check

Sequencing Months

Use the clues to name the month.

1. This month comes before April. This month begins with the letter J. What is the month?

   _____

2. This month ends with the letter R. This month comes just before December. What is the month?

   _____

3. This month comes before the eighth month but after the fifth month. It ends with the letter Y. What is the month?

   _____

4. This month begins with the letter A. This month is not the eighth month. This month is just before May. What is the month?

   _____

5. This month is 2 months before the eleventh month. This month is just after August. What is the month?

   _____

6. The name of this month has 4 letters. This month is four months before October. What is the month?

   _____

Mark the correct answer.

7. This month comes between September and December. This month does not begin with the letter N.

   ○ January

   ○ August

   ○ October

   ○ November

8. This is the shortest month of the year. It comes between January and April. It has 8 letters in it's name.

   ○ September

   ○ November

   ○ December

   ○ February

Name _____

Understand Plan Solve Check

Dates on a calendar

Use the calendar to answer the questions.

April						
Sunday	Monday	Tuesday	Wednesday	Thursday	Friday	Saturday
	1	2	3	4	5	6
7	8	9	10	11	12	13
14	15	16	17	18	19	20
21	22	23	24	25	26	27
28	29	30				

1. Kara's first softball game is April 12. The next game is 11 days later. On what date is the next game?

   _____

2. Anna's piano recital is on the third Friday. Kate's recital is 8 days after Anna's. On what date is Kate's recital?

   _____

3. The first day of spring vacation is April 8. Students return to school 10 days later. What is the day and date that students return to school?

   _____

   _____

4. Mona's soccer game is on the fourth Saturday. The soccer game before that was 12 days earlier. What are the dates of both games?

   _____

Mark the correct answer.

5. Jason's next piano lesson is 8 days after the first Wednesday. On what date is Jason's next lesson?

   ○ April 10   ○ April 12
   ○ April 11   ○ April 15

6. Victor's next football game is a day before the last Monday. On what date is Victor's next game?

   ○ April 22   ○ April 27
   ○ April 25   ○ April 28

Name _____

Understand　Plan　Solve　Check

Days, Weeks, Months, Years

Use the clues to name the amount of time.

I. Miko's family goes on vacation for less than 3 weeks. Their vacation lasts more than 19 days. How many days is their vacation?

_____ days

2. Andy's baby brother is less than 1 year old. He is more than 10 months old. How many months old is Andy's brother?

_____ months

3. Alex's friend came to visit for more than 13 days. He visited for less than 15 days. How many weeks was the visit?

_____ weeks

4. Mary has lived in her house for less than 25 months. She has lived in her house for more than 23 months. How many years has Mary lived in her house?

_____ years

5. Arlene has been on the swim team for more than 1 month. She has been on the swim team for less than 6 weeks. How many weeks has Arlene been on the swim team?

_____ weeks

6. Anwar has been playing piano for more than 1 year. He has been playing for less than 14 months. How many months has Anwar been playing piano?

_____ months

Mark the correct answer.

7. A week more than 1 month is about _____?

○ 14 days　　○ 8 weeks

○ 5 weeks　　○ 100 days

8. 53 weeks are a little more than _____?

○ 10 weeks　　○ 1 year

○ 6 months　　○ 2 years

PS84　Problem Solving

Name _____

Estimate Time

Circle the best answer.

I. The Chin family is eating dinner right now. About how long will it take?

  ⟨20 minutes⟩   20 hours

2. Sam will mow the lawn today. About how long will it take him?

  30 minutes   30 days

---

3. Jenna's baseball team has a game today. About how long will the game take?

  2 hours   2 days

4. Melba's favorite TV show is starting. About how long is the show?

  I second   I hour

---

5. Carmen is listening to her favorite tape. About how long will it take for her to listen to it?

  60 minutes   60 hours

6. Raymond's family is going on vacation. About how long will they be gone?

  10 days   10 years

Mark the correct answer.

7. About how long would it take to drive cross country?

  ○ 5 minutes

  ○ 5 days

  ○ 5 seconds

  ○ 5 years

8. About how long would it take to see a movie?

  ○ 2 hours

  ○ 2 months

  ○ 2 weeks

  ○ 2 seconds

Reading Strategy • Use Graphic Aids

Laura will be at a picnic all day on the second Friday of the month. She has a soccer game on the fourth Friday of the month. Can she take a dance lesson during the day on June 9?

June						
Sunday	Monday	Tuesday	Wednesday	Thursday	Friday	Saturday
				1	2	3
4	5	6	7	8	9	10
11	12	13	14	15	16	17
18	19	20	21	22	23	24
25	26	27	28	29	30	

What is the date of the second Friday?

June 9

What is the date of the fourth Friday?

June 23

no

Can Laura take a dance lesson on June 9? Why?

She has a picnic.

Use the calendar to solve.

1. Jacob has baseball practice on June 6, 13, and 20. What day of the week does Jacob have baseball practice?

_____

2. Megan has piano lessons every Thursday. On what date is her last lesson in June?

_____

3. Grace is going to a movie from noon until 3 P.M. on the third Saturday of the month. Can she visit her friend Mary at 1 P.M. on June 17? Why or why not?

_____

4. Tom has play practice all day on June 15. Can he go to a party during the day on the third Thursday of the month? Why or why not?

_____

Understand Plan Solve Check

Reading Strategy: Use Graphic Aids

You can use pictures, charts, and graphs to help you solve problems.

Mr. Dala's class sold T-shirts for the school. Four children sold the most shirts. How many more shirts did Perry sell than Anna?

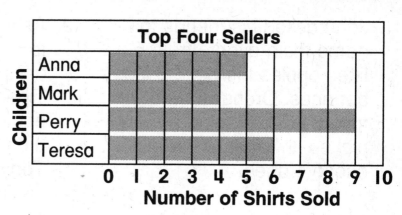

Use the bar graph to help you solve the problem.

How many T-shirts did Perry sell? ___9___

How many T-shirts did Anna sell? ___5___

How many more T-shirts did Perry sell than Anna? _9 — 5 = 4_

Perry sold __4__ more T-shirts.

Use the bar graph to solve.

1. Miss Wallace's class collected box tops. Who collected the most box tops?

   _____

2. Who collected the fewest box tops?

   _____

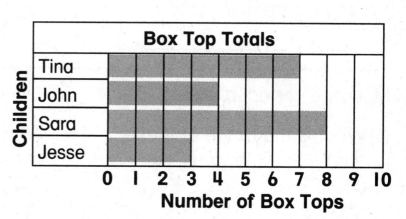

3. How many more box tops did Sara collect than John?

   _____

4. Who collected the second largest number of box tops?

   _____

Name _____

Understand   Plan   Solve   Check

Range, Median, and Mode

Find the range, median, and mode for each group of numbers.

1. John asked his friends to name their favorite fruit. 5 liked apples the best. 3 liked bananas. Oranges were the favorite of 5 friends. 1 friend picked kiwi fruit. 2 friends chose grapes.

   range   median mode

   _____   _____   _____

2. Ashley asked her classmates to name their favorite zoo animal. 11 chose monkeys. Tigers and elephants each were chosen 6 times. 3 children liked giraffes best. Tony said the iguana was his favorite.

   range   median mode

   _____   _____   _____

3. Jim asked his classmates to name their favorite subject at school. 9 children chose art. 4 liked music. Another 4 children chose math. 5 liked science and 2 liked reading.

   range   median mode

   _____   _____   _____

4. Kishi asked 20 people to name their favorite color. 3 people chose red. 6 people liked blue. Green was the favorite of 7 people. 3 liked yellow, and 1 liked orange.

   range   median mode

   _____   _____   _____

Mark the correct answer.

5. What is the range of these numbers? 3, 5, 5, 7, 10

   ○ 3   ○ 7

   ○ 5   ○ 10

6. What is the mode of these numbers? 5, 8, 8, 10, 12

   ○ 5   ○ 10

   ○ 8   ○ 12

Name _____

Algebra: Locate Points on a Grid

The grid shows places at the zoo.
Use the grid to answer the questions.

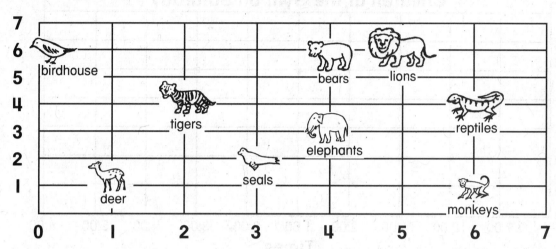

1. Go right 1. Go up 1.
   What is located there?

   _____

2. Go right 5. Go up 6.
   What is located there?

   _____

3. Go right 2. Go up 4.
   What is located there?

   _____

4. Go right 6. Go up 1.
   What is located there?

   _____

5. Go right 3. Go up 2.
   What is located there?

   _____

6. Go right 4, Go up 6.
   What is located there?

   _____

Mark the correct answer.

7. Go right 0. Go up 6.
   What is located there?

   ○ birdhouse

   ○ elephants

   ○ monkeys

   ○ seals

8. Go right 4. Go up 3.
   What is located there?

   ○ birdhouse

   ○ elephants

   ○ reptiles

   ○ lions

Problem Solving   PS89

(Understand) (Plan) (Solve) (Check)

Read Line Graphs

Answer the questions and complete the line graph.

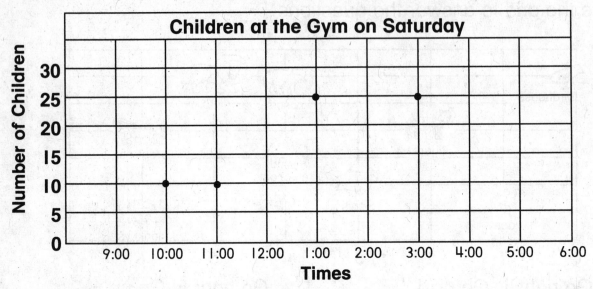

1. At 4:00, there were 20 more children than at 11:00. How many children were at the gym at 4:00?

__30__ children

2. There were 5 fewer children at 12:00 than at 1:00. How many children were at the gym at 12:00?

_____ children

3. There were twice as many children at 2:00 as at 10:00. How many children were at the gym at 2:00?

_____ children

4. The same number of children were at the gym at 5:00 and 10:00. How many children were there at 5:00?

_____ children

Mark the correct answer.

5. There were 5 fewer children at 9:00 than at 5:00. How many children were at the gym at 9:00?

○ 5   ○ 10

○ 15   ○ 20

6. There were 5 more children at 6:00 than at 9:00. How many children were at the gym at 6:00?

○ 5   ○ 10

○ 15   ○ 20

Reading Strategy: Make Predictions

Sometimes you will be asked to make a prediction based on a smaller group.

Tanya's aunt gave her a bag filled with quarters, dimes, nickels, and pennies. Tanya sorted a handful of coins. What prediction can she make about which coin there is the most of in the bag?

Coins Tanya Sorted	
Coin	Tally
quarter	||
dime	ⅢⅠ
nickel	|||
penny	ⅢⅠ ⅢⅠ

1. Compare the number of coins.

   quarters __2__ dimes __5__

   nickels __3__ Pennies __10__

2. Which coin is there the most of? __penny__

3. Which coin is there likely to be the most of in the bag?

   __penny__

___

Look at the tally table. Make a prediction.

4. Jamie grabbed a handful of marbles out of a bag. What prediction can he make about which color marble there are the fewest of?

   Prediction: _____

   _____

Marbles in the Bag	
Color	Tally
blue	ⅢⅠ Ⅰ
red	||
green	ⅢⅠ
yellow	|||

5. What prediction can Jamie make about which color marble there are the most of?

   Prediction: _____

   _____

Interpreting Outcomes of Games

Solve.

1. Kamal made a spinner for which blue or red could be an outcome. Draw and color to show what Kamal's spinner might look like.

2. Ken made a spinner for which the outcome red occurred more often. Draw and color to show what Ken's spinner might look like.

3. Jani made a spinner for which orange is one of three possible outcomes. Draw and color to show what Jani's spinner might look like.

Mark the correct answer.

4. How many times was green the outcome?

○ 4   ○ 9

○ 5   ○ 14

5. Which outcome occurred more often?

○ blue   ○ red

○ green   ○ yellow

Outcomes of Spins	
Color	Tally
green	卌
yellow	卌 IIII

Name _____

Certain or Impossible

Circle **Yes** or **No**.

1. Sue has a bag with 14 green .
   Is pulling a green cube from the bag
   a certain outcome?   **yes**   **no**

2. Is pulling a yellow cube from Sue's
   bag an impossible outcome?   **yes**   **no**

3. Now Sue adds 3 yellow cubes to her
   bag. Is pulling a green cube a certain
   outcome?   **yes**   **no**

4. Is pulling a yellow cube a certain
   outcome?   **yes**   **no**

5. Is pulling a yellow cube an
   impossible outcome?   **yes**   **no**

6. How can you change the cubes in
   Sue's bag so that pulling a yellow
   cube is certain?   _____

Mark the correct answer.

7.

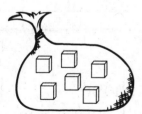

Which is a certain outcome?

○ pull a red cube

○ pull a gray cube

○ pull a white cube

8.

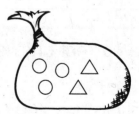

Which is an impossible
outcome?

○ pull a circle

○ pull a square

○ pull a triangle

Understand Plan Solve Check

Likely and Unlikely

Solve.

1. Kayla has a bag with 8 squares and 2 triangles. Is she likely or unlikely to pull a square?

   _____

2. Van has a bag with 7 yellow cubes and 1 orange cube. Is he likely or unlikely to pull an orange cube?

   _____

3. Mike has a bag with 6 triangles and 2 squares. Mason has a bag with 5 squares and 1 triangle. Who is more likely to pull a triangle?

   _____

4. Faith has a bowl with 4 blue cubes and 1 yellow cube. Andy has a bowl with 5 yellow cubes and 2 blue cubes. Who is more likely to pull a blue cube?

   _____

5. Ruben is pulling a cube from a bowl with 5 yellow cubes, 3 green cubes, and 8 red cubes. Which color is Ruben likely to pull?

   _____

6. Elena has a bag with 3 triangles, 7 circles, and 4 squares. Which shape is she likely to pull?

   _____

Mark the correct answer.

7. Which cube is likely to be pulled from the bag?

   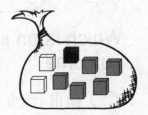

   ○ gray

   ○ white

   ○ black

8. Which shape is likely to be pulled from the bag?

   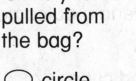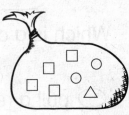

   ○ circle

   ○ square

   ○ triangle

Likelihood of Events

Solve.

1. John has a bowl with 6 circles, 2 triangles, and 3 squares. Which shape is he most likely to pull from the bowl?

_____

2. Judy has a bag with 2 green marbles and 8 blue marbles. Which color is she more likely to pull from the bag?

_____

3. Cody has a drawer with 2 blue T-shirts, 1 white T-shirt, and 6 green T-shirts. If Cody grabs a T-shirt without looking, what color is it most likely to be?

_____

4. Paula has a bag with 3 orange cubes and 7 blue cubes. Devin has a bag with 2 blue cubes and 6 orange cubes. Who is less likely to pull a blue cube?

_____

5. Sara has a drawer with 6 pairs of white socks, 4 pairs of yellow socks, and 2 pairs of blue socks. If Sara grabs a pair of socks without looking, what color is it most likely to be?

_____

6. Tim has 1 penny, 2 dimes, and 6 nickels in his pocket. If he takes out a coin without looking, what is it most likely to be?

_____

Mark the correct answer.

7. Pulling a circle is _____.

○ most likely

○ least likely

○ certain

○ impossible

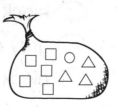

8. Pulling a triangle is _____.

○ most likely

○ least likely

○ more likely

○ less likely

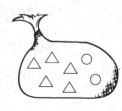

Name _____

Equally Likely

Use the bag of shapes to answer the questions.

1. What could you change to make pulling a square and a triangle equally likely?

_____

_____

2. What could you change to make pulling a square less likely than pulling a circle?

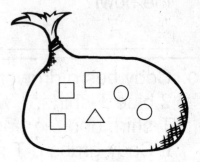

_____

_____

3. What could you change to make pulling a triangle more likely than pulling a square?

_____

_____

Mark the correct answer.

4.

Which shapes are you equally likely to spin?

○ triangle and square

○ square and circle

○ triangle and circle

○ circle and rectangle

5.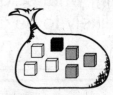

Which colors are equally likely to be pulled?

○ black and gray

○ gray and white

○ black and white

Name _____

Understand Plan Solve Check

Reading Strategy: Use Graphic Aids

Sometimes using a table or chart makes
it easier to solve problems.

Nolan put the following shapes in a bag:
square, circle, circle, triangle, square, triangle,
square, circle, circle, circle, triangle, circle,
circle, triangle, triangle. Which shape is
most likely to be pulled?

1. Complete the tally table.

2. Look at the table. Which
   shape is most likely to be
   pulled from the bag?

   circle
   _____

Shapes in the Bag	
Shape	**Tally**
circle	⦀⦀ ⦀⦀
square	
triangle	

Make a table to solve.

3. Shelly put these shapes in a
   bag: circle, square, circle,
   circle, square, square,
   square, circle, square, and
   square. Which shape is
   more likely to be pulled?

Shapes in the Bag	
Shape	**Tally**
circles	
squares	

A _____ is more likely to
be pulled.

4. Rico put these cubes in a
   box: blue, yellow, red, red,
   yellow, red, blue, red, yellow,
   yellow, red, blue, red, and
   red. Which color is most
   likely to be pulled?

Cubes in the Box	
Color	**Tally**
yellow	
red	
blue	

_____ is most likely to
be pulled.

Name _____

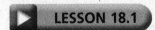

Understand   Plan   Solve   Check

Plane Shapes

Circle the correct shape.

1. Jerry is drawing a picture.
   He draws a circle for the sun.
   Which shape does he draw?

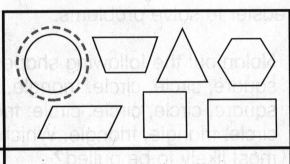

2. Meg is drawing a picture.
   She draws a triangle for a tree.
   Which shape does she draw?

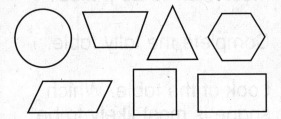

3. Marty is drawing a picture.
   He draws a trapezoid for a boat.
   Which shape does he draw?

4. Lori is drawing a picture. She
   draws a square for a window.
   Which shape does she draw?

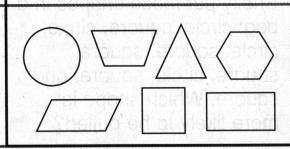

Mark the correct answer.

5. Which is a hexagon?

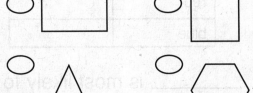
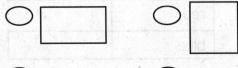

6. Which is a parallelogram?

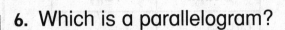

Name _____

Understand   Plan   Solve   Check

Algebra: Sort Plane Shapes

Solve.

1. Sika has a right triangle, a circle, a square, and a rectangle. Which shape does not belong in a group named "Shapes with Square Corners"?

_____

2. Taka has a hexagon, a triangle, a parallelogram, and a trapezoid. Which shape does not belong to a group named "Shapes with More Than 3 Angles"?

_____

3. Ramon has a trapezoid, a hexagon, a square, and a parallelogram. Which shape does not belong to a group named "Shapes with 4 Sides"?

_____

4. Cody has a hexagon, a trapezoid, a rectangle, and a parallelogram. Which shape does not belong to a group named "Shapes with No Square Corners"?

_____

5. April has a rectangle, a trapezoid, and a square. Circle the name she can give her group of shapes.

Shapes with More Than 3 Sides

Shapes with 3 Angles

6. Rosa has a trapezoid, a parallelogram, and a rectangle. Circle the name she can give her group of shapes.

Shapes with Less Than 4 Sides

Shapes with 4 Angles

Mark the correct answer.

7. What shape **does not** belong in the group "Shapes with Angles"?

○ hexagon
○ circle
○ parallelogram

8. What shape **does** belong in the group "Shapes with More Than 4 Sides"?

○ triangle
○ rectangle
○ hexagon

Combine and Separate Shapes

Circle the shape.

1. Tony has 2 triangles that are the same size and shape. What other shape could he make with the 2 triangles?

2. Norma has 3 parallelograms that are all the same shape and size. What other shape could she make with the 3 parallelograms?

3. Kim has 3 triangles that are all the same shape and size. What other shape could she make with the 3 triangles?

4. Scott has 3 triangles that are all the same size and shape. He also has 1 trapezoid. What other shape could he make with the triangles and trapezoid?

Mark the correct answer.

5. Which shapes can be used to make a trapezoid?
   - ○ 3 triangles
   - ○ 2 hexagons
   - ○ 2 rectangles
   - ○ 3 squares

6. Which shapes can be used to make a hexagon?
   - ○ 2 squares
   - ○ 2 parallelograms
   - ○ 2 triangles
   - ○ 2 trapezoids

Name _____

Understand Plan Solve Check

Reading Strategy • Create Mental Images

Ollie has 6 parallelograms.
How many hexagons can he make?

Picture the problem.

**Think about what you
need to model.**

Ollie has
6 parallelograms.

Ollie needs
3 parallelograms to
make 1 hexagon.

Solve.   Ollie needs ____3____ parallelograms for each hexagon.

Ollie can make ____2____ hexagons.

Picture the problems.
Then solve.

1. Fran has 8 trapezoids all the same size and shape. How many hexagons can she make with the 8 trapezoids? _____ hexagons	2. Shari has 2 squares that are the same size. She puts them together one above the other. What shape does she make? _____
3. Frank has 12 triangles all the same shape and size. How many hexagons can he make with the 12 triangles? _____ hexagons	4. Joe has 8 triangles all the same size and shape. How many rectangles can he make with the 8 triangles? _____ rectangles

Reading Strategy   PS101

Solid Figures

Write the name of the solid figure.

rectangular prism

cone

cube

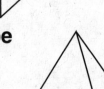
cylinder   **pyramid**

sphere

---

1. I am a can.
I am a drum.
What solid figure am I?

cylinder

2. I am a tepee.
I am a party hat.
What solid figure am I?

_____

---

3. I am a globe.
I am a beach ball.
What solid figure am I?

_____

4. I am a shoe box.
I am a book.
What solid figure am I?

_____

Mark the correct answer.

5. Which object is shaped like this solid figure?

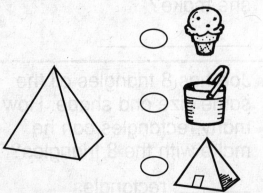

6. Which object has the same shape as this solid figure?

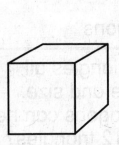

Understand **Plan** **Solve** **Check**

Algebra: Sort Solid Figures

Circle the correct figures using the descriptions.

1. 0 faces, 0 edges, 0 vertices

2. 6 faces, 12 edges, 8 vertices

3. 5 faces, 8 edges, 5 vertices

Mark the correct answer.

4. There is a figure with 5 faces, 8 edges, and 5 vertices. Which is it?

 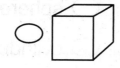

5. There is a figure with 6 faces, 12 edges, and 8 vertices. Which is it?

 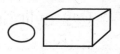

Name _____

Compare Solid Figures and Plane Shapes

Write the name of the solid figure.

1. Taj drew around the faces of his
   solid figure. He drew 6 squares.
   What solid figure does Taj have? _____

2. Kyoko drew around the faces of her
   solid figure. She drew 6 rectangles.
   What solid figure does Kyoko have? _____

3. Ken drew around the faces of his solid figure.
   He drew I square and 4 triangles.
   What solid figure does Ken have? _____

4. Dena could not draw around the
   face of her solid figure.
   What solid figure does Dena have? _____

Mark the correct answer.

5. Anna's solid figure does not
   have any faces to draw.
   What figure does she have?

   ○ cube

   ○ sphere

   ○ cone

   ○ cylinder

6. Bo has two solid figures.
   They each have a square for
   one of their faces. Which
   two figures could she have?

   ○ pyramid and cube

   ○ rectangular prism and
     cone

   ○ sphere and cube

   ○ cylinder and pyramid

Understand   Plan   Solve   Check

Reading Strategy: Use Graphic Aids

Sometimes you can use a table, chart, or graph to help you solve problems. Tables, charts, and graphs are called graphic aids.

This table shows the number of faces for each solid figure.

Number of Shapes Needed for Solid Figures			
solid figure	squares	rectangles	triangles
cube	6	0	0
sphere	0	0	0
pyramid	1	0	4
rectangular prism	0	6	0
total	7	6	4

Use the information in the table to complete each problem.

1. A cube has ____6____ square faces.

_____

2. A rectangular prism has _____ rectangular faces.

_____

3. A pyramid has _____ square face and

_____ triangular faces.

_____

4. A _____ has 0 faces.

_____

5. A _____ has 5 faces.

Congruence

Circle the correct answer.

1. Lily made 2 congruent triangles. Which triangles did Lily make?

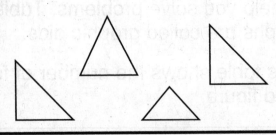

2. Ryan drew 2 congruent leaves. Which leaves did Ryan draw?

3. Karla finds 2 congruent seashells. Which seashells does Karla find?

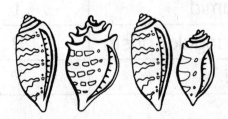

4. Tony has 2 congruent heart shapes. Which shapes does Tony have?

Mark the correct answer.

5. Which figure is congruent to ?

6. Which figure is congruent to ?

Name _____

Understand Plan Solve Check

Symmetry

Circle the correct answer.

1. Peter drew a moon with a line of symmetry. Which moon did he draw?	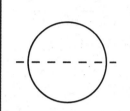
2. Kerri drew a rocket with a line of symmetry. Which rocket did she draw?	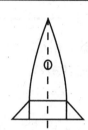 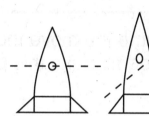
3. Alice drew a number with a line of symmetry. Which number did she draw?	 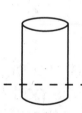 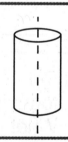
4. Albert drew a jar with a line of symmetry. Which jar did he draw?	  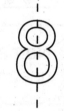

Mark the correct answer.

5. Which letter has a line of symmetry?

6. Which picture has a line of symmetry?

Understand • Plan • Solve • Check

Slides, Flips, and Turns

Solve.

1. Name the move that Ted used to make this pattern.

    flip

   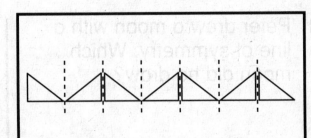

2. Name the move that Jill used to make this pattern.

   _____

   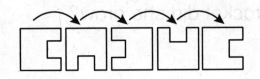

3. Name the move that Joyce used to make this pattern.

   _____

   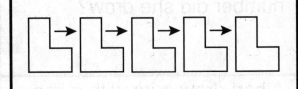

4. Pete used two different moves to make this pattern. What were they?

   _____ and _____

   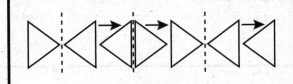

Mark the correct answer.

5. Which word names the move?

   3 → 3

   ○ turn
   ○ flip
   ○ slide

6. Which word names the move?

   5 → ៦

   ○ turn
   ○ flip
   ○ slide

Reading Strategy: Make a Prediction

Sometimes you can make a prediction based on what you already know.

Jenna predicts that this figure has a line of symmetry. Is Jenna's prediction correct?

Can you divide the figure into two congruent figures? Draw a line to find out.

The figure has a line of symmetry. Jenna's prediction is correct.

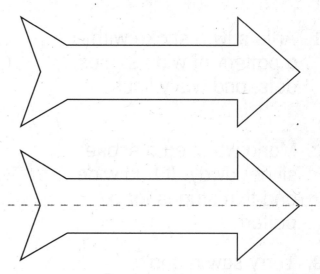

Make a prediction. Then draw the line of symmetry if that is what you predicted.

1. Does this figure have a line of symmetry? Circle your prediction.
Prediction: yes   no

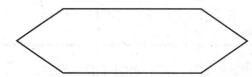

---

2. Does this figure have a line of symmetry? Circle your prediction.
Prediction: yes   no

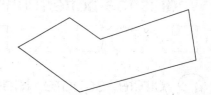

---

3. Does this figure have a line of symmetry? Circle your prediction.
Prediction: yes   no

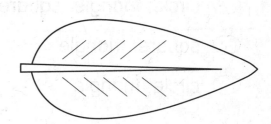

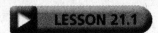

Understand Plan Solve Check

Algebra: Describe Patterns

Draw lines to match the pattern to the snake.
Circle the pattern unit on each snake.

1. Artie saw a snake with a pattern of wide stripes, dots, and wavy lines.

A.

2. Maria watched a snake slither away. It had wide and thin stripes for a pattern.

B.

3. Terry saw a snake with a pattern of thin stripes, wavy lines, and diamonds.

C.

4. A snake crawled under a rock. It had three dots, wide stripes, and thin stripes for a pattern.

D.

Mark the correct answer.

5. What is the pattern unit?

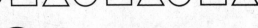

- ○ circle, square, triangle
- ○ circle, triangle, square
- ○ square, triangle
- ○ circle, triangle

6. What is the pattern unit?

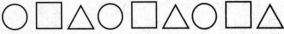

- ○ wavy line, dot
- ○ straight line, diamond
- ○ wavy line, straight line, dot
- ○ straight line, wavy line

Name _____

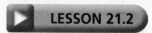

Understand Plan Solve Check

Algebra: Extend Pattern Units

Use your 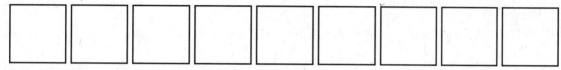.
Follow the directions.

1. Color the first square red. Color the second square yellow.
Color the third square blue. Repeat the pattern.

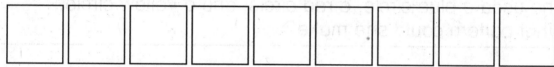

2. Color the third square blue. Color the first square green.
Color the second square purple. Repeat to extend the pattern.

3. Color the fourth circle red. Color the second circle green.
Color the first circle orange. Color the third circle yellow.
Repeat to extend the pattern.

Mark the correct answer.

4. What is the pattern unit?

○

○

○

○

5. What is the pattern unit?

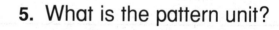

○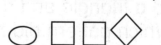

○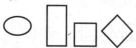

○

○

Problem Solving PS111

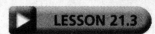

Algebra: Make Patterns

Make the pattern. Circle the pattern unit.

1. James made a pattern unit.
   He used a square and a circle.
   What pattern could he make?

2. Tina made a pattern unit.
   She used a blue circle, a red circle, and a yellow circle.
   What pattern could she make?

3. Mario made a pattern unit.
   He used a blue square, a circle, and a yellow square.
   What pattern could he make?

Mark the correct answer.

4. Tony used a triangle and a square. Which pattern did he make?

   ○ △□△□△□

   ○ ○□○□○□

   ○ △▽△▽△▽

   ○ □○□○□○

5. Rachel used a circle, a triangle, and a square. Which pattern did she make?

   ○ ○△○△○△

   ○ △○□△○□△○□

   ○ □○□○□○

   ○ □△□△□△

Name _____

Reading Strategy: Make a Prediction

Sometimes you need to make a prediction in order to solve a problem. Use what you know to make your prediction.

Mario made this pattern with shapes.
Predict which shape he will draw next.

1. What pattern unit did Mario use? _____

2. What part of the pattern unit is missing at the end of Mario's pattern? _____

3. Predict what the next shape will be. _____

Predict what comes next.

4. Predict the next shape in this pattern.

   Pattern unit _____

   Prediction _____

---

5. Predict the next two shapes in this pattern.

   Pattern unit _____

   Prediction _____

Name _____

Understand Plan Solve Check

Reading Strategy • Create Mental Images

Sometimes you can create a picture in
your mind to help you solve problems.

Jake made this pattern. He made a mistake.
Find the mistake Jake made and correct it.

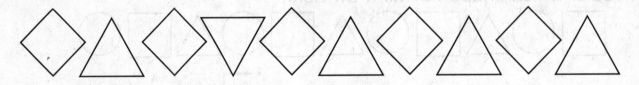

Picture the pattern unit.

**Keep the pattern unit in mind. Look for the mistake in
the pattern.**

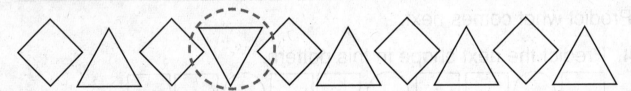

Correct the mistake.

Picture the pattern unit in your mind.
Circle the mistake and correct it.

1.

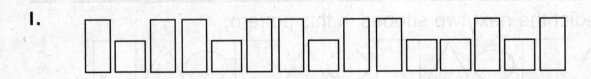

2. | 3 9 | 3 3 | 3 9 | 3 9

9

Measure Length with Nonstandard Units

Measure with the given unit.

1. About how far is it from your desk to the 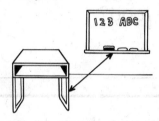? Measure in footsteps.

about _____ footsteps

2. About how wide is your chair? Measure in paper clips.

about _____ paper clips

3. About how long is the . Measure in bags.

about _____ bags

4. About how high is your math book? Measure in paper clips.

about _____ paper clips

Mark the correct answer.

5. About how many paper clips long is the ribbon?

- ⃝ about 1 paper clip
- ⃝ about 2 paper clips
- ⃝ about 3 paper clips
- ⃝ about 4 paper clips

6. About how many paper clips long is the string?

- ⃝ about 1 paper clip
- ⃝ about 2 paper clips
- ⃝ about 3 paper clips
- ⃝ about 4 paper clips

Name _____

Understand   Plan   Solve   Check

Length and Distance

Solve.

1. Mary has a toy dog 6 paper clips tall. Jared has a toy dog 8 paper clips tall. Who has the taller dog?

   _____

2. Mark built a road 14 blocks long. Brad built a road 24 blocks long. Who built the longer road?

   _____

3. Anita made three beaded necklaces using the same size beads. The necklaces have 12 beads, 24 beads, and 18 beads. Put the necklaces in order from longest to shortest.

   _____

   _____

4. Ryan made three towers using the same size blocks. The towers are 18 blocks tall, 9 blocks tall, and 12 blocks tall. Put the towers in order from shortest to tallest.

   _____

   _____

Mark the correct answer.

5. About how many paper clips long is the ribbon?

   ○ about 1 paper clip
   ○ about 2 paper clips
   ○ about 3 paper clips
   ○ about 4 paper clips

6. About how many paper clips long is the string?

   ○ about 1 paper clip
   ○ about 2 paper clips
   ○ about 3 paper clips
   ○ about 4 paper clips

Understand Plan Solve Check

Measure to the Nearest Inch

Measure to the nearest inch.

1. Greg has a paintbrush. He knows it is more than 6 inches long. About how long is a paintbrush?

about _____ inches

2. Karen has a snap cube. She knows it is less than six inches long. About how many inches long is a snap cube?

about _____ inches

3. Rosa uses an inch ruler to measure the length of her shoe. About how many inches long is a shoe?

about _____ inches

4. Len has a marker. He used an inch ruler to measure how long it is. About how many inches long is a marker?

about _____ inches

Mark the correct answer.

5. Think about the real object. About how long is it?

○ about 1 inch
○ about 2 inches
○ about 5 inches
○ about 12 inches

6. Think about the real object. About how long is it?

○ about 20 inches
○ about 18 inches
○ about 12 inches
○ about 6 inches

Name _____

Inch, Foot, and Yard

Think about real objects. Write inches, feet, or yards.

1. Mark measures the length of the canoe.

It is 4 _yards_ long.

2. Kelli measures the length of her whistle.

It is 2 _____ long.

3. Bill measures the width of his sleeping bag.

It is 2 _____ wide.

4. Stacy measures the highest part of the tent.

It is 6 _____ high.

5. Terri measures her hot dog.

It is 4 _____ long.

6. Tim measures a strawberry.

It is 1 _____ long.

Mark the correct answer.

7. Which is the best estimate for the real object?

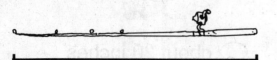

- ○ 6 inches   ○ 2 yards
- ○ 3 inches   ○ 1 foot

8. Which is the best estimate for the real object?

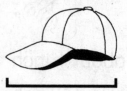

- ○ 3 feet   ○ 2 yards
- ○ 8 inches   ○ 8 feet

Fahrenheit Thermometer

1. How many degrees warmer was it at 2 o'clock?

8 o'clock   **2 o'clock**

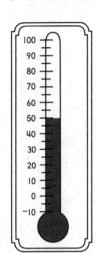 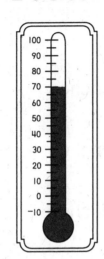

__70__ °F – __50__ °F = __20__ °F

2. The thermometer shows the temperature outside. The temperature inside is 10° warmer. What is the temperature inside?

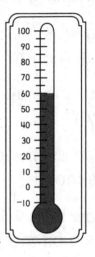

_____ °F + _____ °F = _____ °F

Mark the correct answer.

3. What is the temperature?

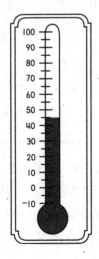

○ 40°F   ○ 41°F

○ 45°F   ○ 55°F

4. What is the temperature?

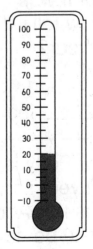

○ 10°F   ○ 20°F

○ 25°F   ○ 30°F

Reading Strategy • Make Predictions

Sometimes a problem will ask you to find out what happens next.

Alan's puppy is 15 inches long.
Last month it was 12 inches long.
About how long will it be next month?

How long was Alan's puppy last month?	__12__ inches
How long is the puppy this month?	__15__ inches
How much did the puppy grow in a month?	__3__ inches
About how long will the puppy be next month?	__15__ + __3__ = __18__ inches

---

Solve to find out what happens next.

1. Chan planted a tree. This year the tree is 6 feet tall. Last year it was 4 feet tall. About how tall will the tree be next year?

about _____ feet tall

2. Ben's tomato plant is 18 inches tall. Last week it was 14 inches tall. About how tall will it be next week?

about _____ inches tall

---

3. This year Patty is 43 inches tall. Last year she was 40 inches tall. About how tall will she be next year?

about _____ inches tall

4. Celia has a new kitten. It is 5 inches tall. Will it be about 5, 12, or 24 inches tall when it is grown up?

about _____ inches tall

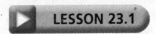

Understand Plan Solve Check

Measure Capacity with Nonstandard Units

Solve.

1. Julia fills a mug with water.
   Barry fills a wading pool with water.
   Who uses more water?

   _____

2. Tami makes a pitcher of lemonade.
   Angie make a glass of lemonade.
   Who makes more lemonade?

   _____

3. Lee has a pail full of water.
   Craig has a pitcher full of water.
   Does Lee or Craig have more water?

   _____

4. Pablo fills a bowl with soup.
   His sister fills a cup with soup.
   Does the cup or the bowl hold
   more soup?

   _____

Mark the correct answer.

5. Which holds more?

6. Which holds less?

Understand   Plan   Solve   Check

Cups, Pints, Quarts, and Gallons

Solve.

1. Abby bought 2 quarts of juice. Sandy bought 3 pints of juice. Who bought more juice?

Abby
_____

2. Jean drank 3 cups of water. Carl drank 1 pint of water. Who drank more water?

_____

3. Rory bought 3 pints of milk. Antoine bought 1 gallon of milk. Who bought more milk?

_____

4. Louis drank 5 cups of juice. Amy drank 1 quart of juice. Who drank more juice?

_____

Mark the correct answer.

5. How many quarts equal 1 gallon?

   ○ 1 quart

   ○ 2 quarts

   ○ 4 quarts

   ○ 8 quarts

6. How many cups equal 3 pints?

   ○ 2 cups

   ○ 3 cups

   ○ 6 cups

   ○ 9 cups

(Understand) (Plan) (Solve) (Check)

Measure Weight with Nonstandard Units

Solve.

1. Kate wants to know if the disk or the shoe is heavier. She puts them on a scale. Does the shoe side or the disk side dip lower?

_____

2. Hanna found a postcard and a golf ball. She used paper clips to weigh them. Did it take more paper clips to weigh the postcard or the golf ball?

_____

3. Luis has a sandwich and a cracker for lunch. He put them on a scale to see which was the heaviest. Did the sandwich side or the cracker side dip lower?

_____

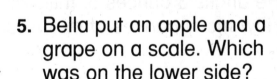

Mark the correct answer.

4. Juan put a baseball and a marble on a scale. Which was on the lower side?

   ○ baseball

   ○ marble

5. Bella put an apple and a grape on a scale. Which was on the lower side?

   ○ apple

   ○ grape

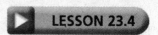

Ounces and Pounds

Solve.

1. Mei's math book is 1 pound.
   Her reading book is 2 pounds.
   How many pounds of books are in her backpack?

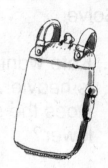

   __3__ pounds

2. Tyrell has a 5-pound cat.
   Jamal has an 8-pound cat.
   How many pounds do their cats weigh together?

   _____ pounds

3. Amy drinks 6 ounces of juice for breakfast.
   She drinks 8 ounces of juice for lunch.
   How many ounces of juice does she drink?

   _____ ounces

4. Alex drinks 8 ounces of milk for breakfast.
   He drinks 8 ounces of milk for dinner.
   How many ounces of milk does he drink?

   _____ ounces

Mark the correct answer.

5. Amy wants to
   know about how
   heavy a suitcase is.

   ◯ about 5 ounces
   ◯ about 5 pounds

Name _____

Reading Strategy • Use Picture Clues

Understand   Plan   Solve   Check

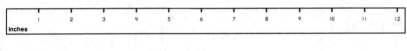

inches

ruler

scale

cup

Fahrenheit

thermometer

Use picture clues to solve.
Write the name of the tool you would use.

1. to find out the temperature on a snowy day   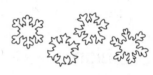   thermometer

2. to find out how much water will fill a bowl   _____

3. to find out the weight of a backpack   _____

4. to find out how long your pencil is      _____

5. to find out the temperature in the freezer   _____

Name _____

Centimeters and Meters

Think about the real objects. Circle the best answer.

1. Jennifer measures the toaster.
   It is about

   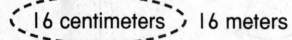 16 meters   high.

2. Mimi measures the table.
   It is about

   3 centimeters   3 meters   long.

   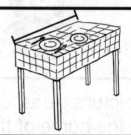

3. Dan measures a cereal box.
   It is about

   25 centimeters   25 meters   high.

4. Dan measures the refrigerator.
   It is about

   2 centimeters   2 meters   high.

Mark the best answer.

5. About how long is a pen?

   ○ about 15 centimeters
   ○ about 15 meters
   ○ about 1 centimeter
   ○ about 1 meter

6. About how tall is a
   milk carton?

   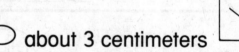

   ○ about 3 centimeters
   ○ about 3 meters
   ○ about 24 centimeters
   ○ about 24 meters

PS126   Problem Solving

Name _____

Milliliters and Liters

Solve.

1. Liz says a drop of water is about 1 milliliter. Dan says it is about 1 liter. Who is right?

_____

2. Peter has a fish tank. He wants to know how much it holds. Will Peter use milliliters or liters to find out?

_____

3. Mr. Chin is getting gas for his car. Does the gas tank hold about 60 milliliters or about 60 liters?

about _____

4. Raul has a spoonful of peanut butter. Does the spoon hold milliliters or liters?

_____

5. Mira wants to fill a watering can with water. Will she need about 4 milliliters or about 4 liters to fill the can?

about _____

6. Kyle wants to measure the amount of orange juice in a pitcher. Will he measure the juice in liters or milliliters?

_____

Mark the correct answer.

7. About how much will an eyedropper hold?

○ about 10 milliliters

○ about 1 liter

○ more than 1 liter

8. How much water will it take to fill a wading pool?

○ about 10 milliliters

○ about 1 liter

○ more than 1 liter

Name _____

LESSON 24.3

Grams and Kilograms

Understand · Plan · Solve · Check

Circle the better answer.

1. An adult cat has a mass of about 6 kilograms. What might be the mass of a kitten?

16 kilograms

(850 grams)

2. A baby elephant has a mass of about 2,000 kilograms. What might be the mass of an adult elephant?

2,000 kilograms

5,000 kilograms

3. A lamb has a mass of about 50 kilograms. What might be the mass of an adult sheep?

150 kilograms

900 kilograms

4. An adult rabbit has a mass of about 1 kilogram. What might be the mass of a baby rabbit?

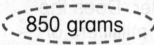

1 kilogram

100 grams

Mark the correct answer.

5. Would you measure the mass of a baby mouse in grams or kilograms?

○ grams

○ kilograms

6. Would you measure the mass of a human baby in grams or kilograms?

○ grams

○ kilograms

PS128   Problem Solving

Understand   Plan   Solve   Check

Celsius Thermometer

1. Rico looks out the window. It is a cold, rainy day. Rico checks the thermometer. Is the temperature 5°C or 25°C?

   _____

2. Ruby says it is a good day for building a snowman. She looks at the thermometer. Is the temperature 0°C or 38°C?

   _____

3. Luisa and her friends are going outside to the pool. Luisa checks the temperature. is the temperature 0°C or 32°C?

   _____

4. Jody is going for a walk. His mother says it is 34°C outside. Will Jody wear a coat or a T-shirt?

   _____

5. Martha says that 40°C is a very hot day. Tony says it is a cold day. Who is right?

   _____

6. The thermometer shows 18°C. Steve wants to round the temperature to the nearest ten degrees. What does he say the temperature is?

   _____

Mark the correct answer.

7. What temperature is it?

   ○ 10°C
   ○ 15°C
   ○ 18°C
   ○ 22°C

8. What temperature is it?

   ○ 17°C
   ○ 24°C
   ○ 30°C
   ○ 33°C

   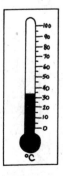

Name _____

   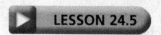

Understand   Plan   Solve   Check

Reading Strategy • Use Picture Clues

Using pictures can help you solve problems.

The children are playing outside.
Rosa looks at the thermometer.
Is the temperature 0°C or 33°C?

Look at the picture for clues.

What is the weather like? _____

What are the children wearing? _____

What are the children doing? _____

Solve the problem.
The temperature is _____.

Look for picture clues.
Then circle the better estimate.

1.

    18°C   32°C

2.

    30°C   2°C

3.

    28°C   5°C

4.

    45°C   20°C

Name _____

Understand   Plan   Solve   Check

Perimeter

Solve.

1. Sue drew a square. Each side of the square was 4 centimeters long. What was the perimeter of the square Sue drew?

   _____ centimeters

2. Fred drew a triangle. Two of the sides were 5 centimeters long. One side was 3 centimeters long. What was the perimeter of Fred's triangle?

   _____ centimeters

3. Dante drew a rectangle. Two of the sides were 7 centimeters long. Two of the sides were 2 centimeters long. What was the perimeter of Dante's rectangle?

   _____ centimeters

4. Tina has a garden. Each of the 4 sides is 12 feet long. Tina wants to put a fence around the garden. How much fence will she need?

   _____ feet

5. Cole's room is shaped like a rectangle. Two sides are 12 feet long. Two sides are 10 feet long. What is the perimeter of Cole's room?

   _____ feet

6. Kimi cut a triangle from a piece of paper. Each side of the triangle was 5 inches long. What was the perimeter of Kimi's triangle?

   _____ inches

Mark the correct answer.

7. The side of a square is 3 feet. What is the perimeter?

   ○ 8 feet   ○ 12 feet

   ○ 16 feet   ○ 20 feet

8. One side of a triangle is 2 feet. Two sides are 4 feet. What is the perimeter of the triangle?

   ○ 2 feet   ○ 8 feet

   ○ 10 feet   ○ 12 feet

Name _____

Understand   Plan   Solve   Check

Area

Solve.

1. Marc and Janna each drew a figure. Find the area of each figure. Color the one that has more units.

Marc   Janna

_____ units   _____ units

2. Jeff and Casey each drew a figure. Find the area of each figure. Color the one that has more units.

Jeff   Casey

_____ units   _____ units

3. Amy and Tani each drew a figure. Find the area of each figure. Color the one that has more units.

Amy   Tani

        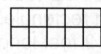

_____ units   _____ units

Find the area.
Mark the correct answer.

4.

○ 8 units   ○ 6 units

○ 4 units   ○ 2 units

5.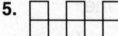

○ 8 units   ○ 6 units

○ 4 units   ○ 2 units

PS132   Problem Solving

Name _____

Reading Strategy • Make Predictions

Kishi wants to know the perimeter of her table. She measures each side. Two sides are 4 feet long. Two sides are 2 feet long. What will Kishi do next to find the perimeter?

add the measurements

What is the perimeter of the table? __12__ feet

Decide what will happen next.
Then solve.

1. Ryan wants to know the perimeter of his room. The room is a square. Ryan measures one side. It is 10 feet long. What does he do next?

_____

What is the perimeter of Ryan's room?

_____ feet

2. Tony wants to find the area of his desk. He covers the desk with tiles. What does Tony do next to find the area of his desk?

_____

Tony uses 18 tiles. What is the area of his desk?

_____ tiles

3. Mika wants to know the perimeter of her garden. She measures each side. Two sides are 10 feet long. Two sides are 8 feet long. What does Mika do next?

_____

What is the perimeter of Mika's garden?

_____ feet

4. Dixie is making a gift for a friend. She wants to know how many tiles she needs to cover it. First she predicts how many. Then what does she do?

_____

Dixie uses 24 tiles. How much area does she cover?

_____ tiles

Name _____

 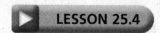
Volume

Solve.

1. Mark has a shoe box. 12 cubes cover the bottom. The box can fit 4 layers of cubes. What is the volume of Mark's shoe box?

_____ cubes

2. April has a box. There are 8 cubes in the bottom layer of the box. The box can fit 2 layers of cubes. What is the volume of the box?

_____ cubes

3. Paul makes a solid figure with cubes. First he makes a row of 3 cubes. Then he puts 3 rows of cubes together. What is the volume of the solid figure Paul makes?

_____ cubes

4. Derek makes a row of 5 cubes. Then he puts another row of 5 cubes on top. What is the volume of the solid figure Derek makes?

_____ cubes

5. Judy makes a tower of cubes. The tower is 4 layers high. Each layer has 6 cubes. What is the volume of the tower Judy makes?

_____ cubes

6. Len wants to find the volume of a container. He covers the bottom with 5 cubes. It takes 5 layers to fill the container. What is the volume?

_____ cubes

Find the volume. Mark the correct answer.

7.

○ 3 cubes   ○ 5 cubes

○ 4 cubes   ○ 6 cubes

8.

○ 6 cubes   ○ 18 cubes

○ 12 cubes   ○ 20 cubes

Unit Fractions

Solve. Write the fraction.

1. Mark divided a square into 4 equal parts. Then he painted one of the parts. How much of the square did Mark paint?

_____ of the square

2. Anna cut a pizza into 5 equal pieces. Then she gave one of the pieces to Rosa. How much of the pizza did Anna give to Rosa?

_____ of the pizza

3. Juan divided a sandwich into 2 equal parts. Then he ate one of the parts. How much of the sandwich did Juan eat?

_____ of the sandwich

4. Chet divided a circle into 8 equal parts. Then he shaded one of the parts. How much of the circle did Chet shade?

_____ of the circle

Mark the correct answer.

5. What is the fraction for the shaded part?

  ○ $\frac{1}{3}$ ○ $\frac{1}{5}$

  ○ $\frac{1}{4}$ ○ $\frac{1}{6}$

6. What is the fraction for the shaded part?

  ○ $\frac{1}{2}$ ○ $\frac{1}{4}$

  ○ $\frac{1}{3}$ ○ $\frac{1}{6}$

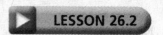
Understand Plan Solve Check

Reading Strategy • Use Picture Clues

Sometimes picture clues can help
you solve a problem.

Kita has 2 rice cakes to share.
She gives $\frac{1}{2}$ of a rice cake to
Kyle. She gives $\frac{1}{3}$ of a rice
cake to Ellen. Who has the
larger piece?

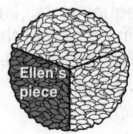

Use the pictures to solve.

Who has the larger piece of rice cake? _____Kyle_____

Use the picture clues to help you solve the problem.

I. Adam has 2 burritos to
share. He gives Mari $\frac{1}{4}$ of
a burrito. He gives Luis $\frac{1}{5}$
of a burrito. Who has the
larger piece?

_____

2. Litsa has 2 corn cakes to
share. She gives $\frac{1}{3}$ of a
corn cake to Debbie. She
gives $\frac{1}{6}$ of a corn cake to
Darren. Who has the larger
piece?

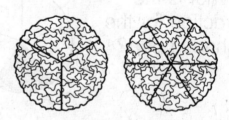

_____

Other Fractions

Color to show the fraction.

1. Amy makes a flag that is $\frac{1}{2}$ red and $\frac{1}{2}$ blue.

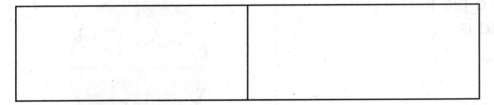

2. Irene makes a flag that is $\frac{1}{4}$ green and $\frac{3}{4}$ yellow.

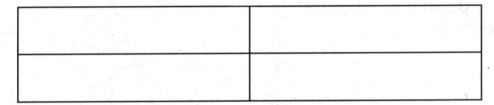

3. Todd makes a flag that is $\frac{1}{3}$ red and $\frac{2}{3}$ yellow.

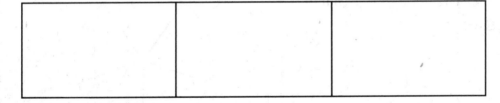

Mark the correct answer.

4. Which fraction matches the picture?

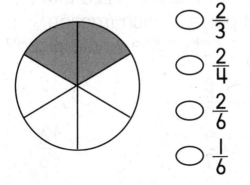

- ○ $\frac{2}{3}$
- ○ $\frac{2}{4}$
- ○ $\frac{2}{6}$
- ○ $\frac{1}{6}$

5. Which fraction matches the picture?

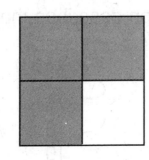

- ○ $\frac{3}{4}$
- ○ $\frac{2}{4}$
- ○ $\frac{1}{4}$
- ○ $\frac{1}{6}$

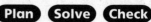

Fractions Equal to 1

Color to show the whole.
Write the fraction that equals the whole.

1. Nora cuts a pie into 4 parts.
Each piece is $\frac{1}{4}$.

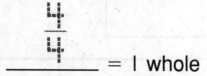

_____ = 1 whole

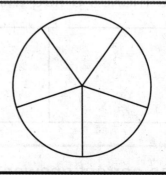

2. Rosa cuts a pizza into 16 parts.
Each piece is $\frac{1}{16}$.

_____ = 1 whole

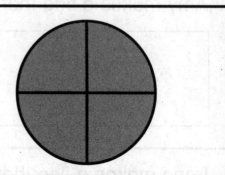

3. Simon cuts a pizza into 5 parts.
Each piece is $\frac{1}{5}$.

_____ = 1 whole

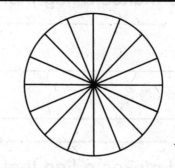

Mark the correct answer.

4. Rick cuts a pizza into 7 parts.
Which fraction describes the
whole pizza?

   ○ $\frac{5}{5}$ ○ $\frac{7}{7}$

   ○ $\frac{8}{8}$ ○ $\frac{10}{10}$

5. Eileen cuts a pizza into
8 parts. Which fraction
describes the whole pizza?

   ○ $\frac{8}{8}$ ○ $\frac{12}{12}$

   ○ $\frac{9}{9}$ ○ $\frac{16}{16}$

Name _____

Understand Plan Solve Check

Unit Fractions of a Group

Solve. Write the fraction.

---

1. There are 6 pizzas at the party. One pizza is sausage. What fraction of the pizzas is the sausage pizza?

_____ of the pizzas

2. There are 12 different drinks at the party. One drink is lemonade. What fraction of the drinks is the lemonade?

_____ of the drinks

---

3. There are 15 chairs at the party. One chair is empty. What fraction of the chairs is the empty chair?

_____ of the chairs

4. There are 7 video games at the party. One game is broken. What fraction of the games is the broken game?

_____ of the games

---

5. There are 5 banners at the party. One of the banners is blue. What fraction of the banners is the blue banner?

_____ of the banners

6. There are 8 presents at the party. One of the presents is open. What fraction of the presents is the open present?

_____ of the presents

Mark the correct answer.

7. What fraction is shaded?

- ○ $\frac{1}{4}$
- ○ $\frac{1}{8}$
- ○ $\frac{1}{6}$
- ○ $\frac{1}{10}$

8. What fraction is shaded?

- ○ $\frac{1}{6}$
- ○ $\frac{1}{11}$
- ○ $\frac{1}{9}$
- ○ $\frac{1}{12}$

Name _____

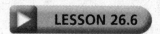

Other Fractions of a Group

Solve. Write the fraction.

1. Lisa has 3 red flowers. Jackie has 2 yellow flowers. What fraction of the flowers are the yellow flowers?

$\frac{2}{5}$

_____ of the flowers

| yellow | yellow | red | red | red |

2. Cory has 4 small toy cars. Robby has 4 big toy cars. What fraction of the toy cars are the small toy cars?

_____ of the toy cars

3. There are 7 dogs. 3 dogs do not have spots. 4 dogs have spots. What fraction of the dogs do **not** have spots?

_____ of the dogs

4. There are 4 children wearing shirts. 1 shirt has stripes. What fraction of the shirts do **not** have stripes?

_____ of the shirts

Mark the correct answer.

5. What fraction is shaded?

○ $\frac{1}{2}$

○ $\frac{1}{3}$

○ $\frac{2}{6}$

○ $\frac{1}{6}$

6. What fraction is white?

○ $\frac{1}{8}$

○ $\frac{2}{6}$

○ $\frac{2}{8}$

○ $\frac{6}{8}$

Hundreds

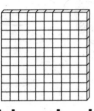   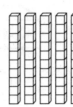 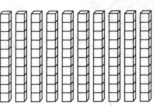   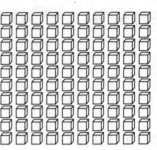

I hundred   =   I0 tens   =   I00 ones

Solve.

I. There are 100 stamps in a sheet. Mr. Vincent buys 900 stamps. How many sheets does he buy?

___9___ sheets

2. There are 100 pencils in a box. The principal buys 3 boxes. How many pencils does he buy?

_____ pencils

3. There are 100 sheets in a pack of paper. Beth buys 5 packs. How many sheets of paper does she buy?

_____ sheets of paper

4. There are 100 paper clips in a box. Mr. Davis buys 700 paper clips. How many boxes does he buy?

_____ boxes

Mark the correct answer.

5. How many tens are there?

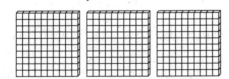

○ 3

○ 30

○ 300

6. How many ones are there?

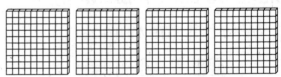

○ 4

○ 40

○ 400

Problem Solving   PS141

Name _____

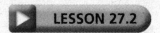

Hundreds, Tens, and Ones

Solve. Use the fewest boxes.

1. Mr. Morris buys safety pins for 238 people. What does he buy?

___2___ boxes of 100   ___3___ boxes of 10   ___8___ single pins

2. Ms. Webster buys 200 safety pins. What does she buy?

_____ boxes of 100   _____ boxes of 10   _____ single pins

3. A teacher buys 404 safety pins. What does she buy?

_____ boxes of 100   _____ boxes of 10   _____ single pins

4. A store owner buys 335 safety pins. What does he buy?

_____ boxes of 100   _____ boxes of 10   _____ single pins

Mark the correct answer.

5. Which is the number?

○ 246   ○ 462

○ 264   ○ 426

6. Which is the number?

○ 423   ○ 324

○ 432   ○ 342

Understand Plan Solve Check

Place Value

Circle the value of the underlined digit.

1. Marty has 6<u>9</u>2 paper clips.

900   (90)   9

2. Maria has 32<u>7</u> books.

700   70   7

3. Kendra has 87<u>1</u> sheets of paper.

100   10   1

4. Rob has 1<u>3</u>8 staples.

300   30   3

5. Angel has 4<u>6</u>3 pencils.

600   60   6

6. Russell has <u>5</u>89 erasers.

500   50   5

Mark the most reasonable estimate.

7. _____ people live in my house.

○ 4
○ 40
○ 400

8. There are _____ children in Miss Smith's class.

○ 2
○ 20
○ 200

Algebra: Different Ways to Show Numbers

Write the number. Then show it a different way.

1. Ara's number has an 8 in the hundreds place. It has a 3 in the ones place and an 8 in the tens place. What is her number?

hundreds	tens	ones

_____

2. Maya's number has a 1 in the tens place. It has a 9 in the ones place and a 2 in the hundreds place. What is her number?

____ + ____ + ____

_____

3. Taro's number has a 4 in the tens place. It has a 1 in the hundreds place and a 2 in the ones place. What is his number?

hundreds	tens	ones

_____

4. Jina's number has a 4 in the ones place. It has a 3 in the tens place and a 9 in the hundreds place. What is her number?

____ hundreds ____ tens ____ ones

_____

Mark the correct answer.

5. six hundred seventy-one

○ 176   ○ 671
○ 617   ○ 761

6. 400 + 4

○ 44   ○ 404
○ 400   ○ 444

Name _____

Reading Strategy • Retell the Story

Sometimes retelling a problem in your
own words can help you solve it.

Jada's mother gives her a 1 dollar bill, 4 dimes, and 3 pennies.
How much money does Jada have?

Retell the problem.

Jada's mother gives her 1 dollar bill, $1.00

4 dimes, $1.10, $1.20, $1.30, $1.40

and 3 pennies. $1.41, $1.42, $1.43

Retell the problem in your own words.
Then solve.

1. Devon has 3 dollar bills and
2 pennies. How much money
does he have?

_____

2. Catelyn has 3 dollar bills,
1 quarter, 1 nickel, and
1 penny. How much does
she have?

_____

3. Ilana's grandfather gives her
1 dollar, 1 quarter, 1 dime,
1 nickel, and 1 penny. How
much money does Ilana
have?

_____

4. Jack has 2 dollar bills,
3 dimes, and 5 pennies.
How much money does
he have?

_____

Name _____

Algebra: Compare Numbers: >, <, and =

Write > or < in the circle.
Solve.

1. There are 562 adults and 652 children at the zoo. Are there more adults or children at the zoo?

562 $<$ 652

children

2. The zoo sold 218 bags of peanuts and 281 bags of popcorn. Were more bags of peanuts or popcorn sold?

218 ◯ 281

_____

3. On Tuesday 716 children visited the park. On Wednesday 709 children visited. On which day did fewer children visit?

716 ◯ 709

_____

4. There are 462 trees in the town park. There are 284 trees in the city park. Are there fewer trees in the town park or the city park?

462 ◯ 284

_____

Mark the correct answer.

5. Choose >, <, or =.

505 ◯ 505

◯ <
◯ >
◯ =

6. Choose > or <.

200 ◯ 20

◯ >
◯ <

Name _____

Understand Plan Solve Check

Missing Numbers to 1,000

Use ▦ , ▭ , and ▫ to show the numbers.
Write the missing numbers.

1. Tara, Simon, Olivia, and Mark got tickets for a show. The numbers were in order. Mark's ticket was number 342. Olivia's ticket was 344. What were the ticket numbers for Tara and Simon?

____	342	____	344
Tara	Mark	Simon	Olivia

2. Four friends ran in a race. Each person was given a number. Tony's number was 287. Julio's number was 290. What were the numbers for Clark and Kelly?

287	____	____	290
Tony	Clark	Kelly	Julio

3. The Broncos basketball team played four games. At each game they scored one more point than before. The last game's score was 112. What were the scores for the other three games?

____	____	____	112
1	2	3	4

4. Jesse, Amy, Tran, and Jim had seats at a play. Their seat numbers were in order. Jesse's seat was number 594. Tran's seat was number 596. What were the other two seat numbers?

594	____	596	____
Jesse	Amy	Tran	Jim

Mark the correct answer.

5. Which number is missing?
   946, 947, _____

   ○ 945   ○ 949
   ○ 948   ○ 950

6. Which number is missing?
   _____, 800, 801

   ○ 803   ○ 799
   ○ 802   ○ 798

Problem Solving PS147

Understand Plan Solve Check

Algebra: Order Numbers on a Number Line

Use the number line to help you.

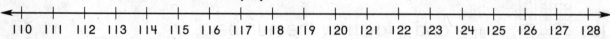

110 111 112 113 114 115 116 117 118 119 120 121 122 123 124 125 126 127 128

---

1. Stacey has 113 crayons. Herbie has 111 crayons. Jonah has 126 crayons. Put the numbers of crayons in order from the least to the greatest.

___111___   ___113___   ___126___

2. Juan has 128 markers. Sue has 115 markers. Joe has 122 markers. Put the numbers of markers in order from the least to the greatest.

_____   _____   _____

---

3. Laurie has 119 stickers. Rochelle has 112 stickers. Sam has 116 stickers. Put the numbers of stickers in order from the least to the greatest.

_____   _____   _____

4. Joan has 110 paper clips. Pat has 126 paper clips. María has 119 paper clips. Put the numbers of paper clips in order from the least to the greatest.

_____   _____   _____

---

5. David has 124 marbles. Ali has 127 marbles. Lynn has 120 marbles. Put the numbers of marbles in order from the least to the greatest.

_____   _____   _____

6. Emily has 117 nuts. Karen has 127 nuts. Carmen has 121 nuts. Put the numbers of nuts in order from the least to the greatest.

_____   _____   _____

Mark the correct answer.

7. Which number is the least?

◯ 120   ◯ 126   ◯ 117

8. Which number is the greatest?

◯ 123   ◯ 128   ◯ 115

Understand Plan Solve Check

Algebra: Find Unknown Numbers on a Number Line

Use the clues.
Show the letter on the number line.
Then read across to solve the riddle.

What can speak every language in the world?

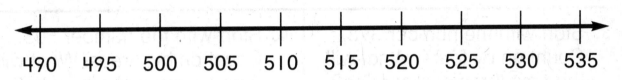

490 495 500 505 510 515 520 525 530 535

I. My tens digit is I.
My hundreds digit is 5
My ones digit is 9.
What number am I? _____

Label me **C** on the number line.

2. My hundreds digit is 4.
My ones digit is 4.
My tens digit is 9.
What number am I? _____

Label me **A** on the number line.

3. I am 10 more than 524.
What number am I? _____

Label me **O** on the number line.

4. I am 20 less than 523.
What number am I? _____

Label me **N** on the number line.

5. I am 10 more than 501.
What number am I? _____

Label me **E** on the number line.

6. I am 20 less than 548.
What number am I? _____

Label me **H** on the number line.

Mark the correct answer.

7. What number is at the dot?

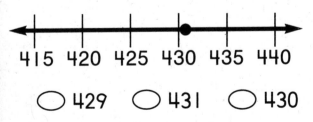

415 420 425 430 435 440

○ 429 ○ 431 ○ 430

8. What number is at the dot?

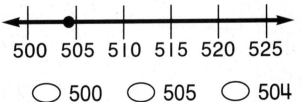

500 505 510 515 520 525

○ 500 ○ 505 ○ 504

Name _____

Algebra: Skip-Count

Skip-count. Write the missing numbers.

1. Start with the number 123. Count on by twos. What will the next three numbers be? 123, _____, _____, _____	**2.** You count by fives and end with 255. What are the first three numbers? _____, _____, _____, 255
3. Start with the number 398. Count on by fours. What will the next three numbers be? 398, _____, _____, _____	**4.** Start with the number 503. Count on by threes. What will the next three numbers be? 503, _____, _____, _____
5. You count by tens and end with 895. What are the first three numbers? _____, _____, _____, 895	**6.** Count on by fives. Start with the number 612. What will the next three numbers be? 612, _____, _____, _____

Mark the correct answer.

7. Which number is missing?

376, 380, _____, 388, 392

○ 382   ○ 385

○ 384   ○ 386

8. Which number is missing?

997, 995, 993, _____, 989

○ 919   ○ 991

○ 988   ○ 999

Understand   Plan   Solve   Check

Reading Strategy • Make Predictions

Sometimes a problem asks you to tell what will happen.

Ben wants to be a better swimmer.
On Monday he swims 3 laps.
On Tuesday he swims 6 laps.
On Wednesday he swims 9 laps.
How many laps will Ben likely swim on Thursday?

Look for a pattern.

laps Ben swam on Monday ___3___

laps Ben swam on Tuesday ___6___

laps Ben swam on Wednesday ___9___

What is the pattern? ___3 more each time___

laps Ben will likely swim on Thursday ___12___

Solve.

1. Mia is learning to knit. She knits 4 rows the first day. She knits 8 rows the second day. She knits 12 rows the third day. How many rows will Mia likely knit on the fourth day?

   _____ rows

2. Jeff is starting to lift weights. He lifts 20 pounds the first month. He lifts 30 pounds the second month. He lifts 40 pounds the third month. How many pounds will Jeff likely lift the fourth month?

   _____ pounds

Name _____

Mental Math: Add Hundreds

Use the addition facts you know to help you solve the problem.

1. Randy counts 400 ants on the playground.
Then he counts 200 ants by the bus stop.
How many ants does he count in all?

$$\begin{array}{r} 400 \\ +\ 200 \\ \hline 600 \end{array}$$

__600__ ants

---

2. Mrs. Brach's room has 300 books.
Mr. Corey's room has 500 books.
How many books are in both
classrooms?

$+$ _____

_____ books

---

3. 100 children sing in the school chorus.
200 children listen to the chorus.
How many children are there in all?

$+$ _____

_____ children

Mark the correct answer.

4. Gina's class sells 600
granola bars and 100 bags
of peanuts. How many
items do they sell in all?

   ◯ 300   ◯ 700
   ◯ 500   ◯ 900

5. At the soccer game, there
are 300 children from Tom's
school and 200 children
from Tami's school. How
many children are at the
game in all?

   ◯ 300   ◯ 500
   ◯ 400   ◯ 600

Model 3-Digit Addition: Regroup Ones

Use ▦ ▭ ◻ .
Add.

1. Mr. Chen ordered 144 bottles of orange juice and 248 bottles of grape juice for his store. How many bottles of juice did he order?

_392_ bottles

2. Mr. Cameron ordered 636 stuffed dogs and 227 stuffed cats for his toy store. How many stuffed animals did he order?

_____ stuffed animals

3. Mrs. Daily ordered 415 red beads and 239 white beads to make jewelry. How many beads did she order?

_____ beads

4. Mr. Hooper ordered 278 roses and 319 daisies for his flower shop. How many flowers did he order?

_____ flowers

Mark the correct answer.

5. Mr. Curtis drove 649 miles one week and 234 miles the next week. How many miles did he drive in all?

○ 873
○ 875
○ 883
○ 973

6. Mrs. Fox drove 168 miles one week and 518 miles the next week. How many miles did she drive in all?

○ 676
○ 678
○ 686
○ 688

Model 3-Digit Addition: Regroup Tens

Add.

1. Mrs. Dehmel read 252 pages in her book on Monday. She read 175 pages on Tuesday. How many pages did she read in the two days?

__427__ pages

2. There are 167 children in Grade 2. There are 165 children in Grade 1. How many children are there in the two grades together?

_____ children

3. Mac watches two movies. The first is 134 minutes long. The second is 185 minutes long. How long are the two movies together?

_____ minutes

4. Dorothy has 426 pennies in one jar. She has 186 pennies in another jar. How many pennies does she have in all?

_____ pennies

Mark the correct answer.

5. Alex has 2 bags of marbles. There are 154 marbles in each bag. How many marbles does he have in all?

○ 154
○ 254
○ 208
○ 308

6. Kristin has 2 sticker books. There are 155 stickers in one book. There are 125 stickers in the other book. How many stickers does she have in all?

○ 318
○ 308
○ 280
○ 218

Mental Math: Subtract Hundreds

Each bundle of paper contains 100 sheets. Solve.

1. April has 7 bundles of paper. She gives 4 to Joe.
   How many sheets of paper does April have left?

   __7__ hundreds − __4__ hundreds = __3__ hundreds

   __700__ − __400__ = __300__

2. Vincent has 4 bundles of paper. He gives 3 to Curt.
   How many sheets of paper does Vincent have left?

   _____ hundreds − _____ hundreds = _____ hundred

   _____ − _____ = _____

3. Farrah has 6 bundles of paper. She gives 2 to Jack.
   How many sheets of paper does Farrah have left?

   _____ hundreds − _____ hundreds = _____ hundreds

   _____ − _____ = _____

Mark the correct answer.

4. Which is the difference?
   $800 - 600 =$ _?_
   - ○ 500
   - ○ 400
   - ○ 300
   - ○ 200

5. Which is the difference?
   5 hundreds − 2 hundreds = _?_
   - ○ 1 hundred
   - ○ 2 hundreds
   - ○ 3 hundreds
   - ○ 4 hundreds

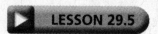

Understand Plan Solve Check

Model 3-Digit Subtraction: Regroup Tens

Use Workmat 5 and [grid] [rod] □ .
Solve.

1. A grizzly bear weighs 582 pounds. A black bear weighs 355 pounds. How many more pounds does the grizzly bear weigh than the black bear?

__227__ more pounds

2. The baby bear weighs 137 pounds. The mother bear weighs 346. How many more pounds does the mother bear weigh than the baby?

_____ pounds

3. A black bear weighs 369 pounds. A polar bear weighs 584 pounds. How many more pounds does the polar bear weigh than the black bear?

_____ pounds

4. The mother polar bear weighs 878 pounds. The baby polar bear weighs 365 pounds. How many more pounds does the mother weigh than the baby?

_____ more pounds

Mark the correct answer.

5. The second grade collected 542 cans of food. The first grade collected 214 cans. How many more cans did the second grade collect than the first grade?

○ 328
○ 332
○ 358
○ 756

6. There are 984 children at East School. There are 738 children at West School. How many more children are there at East School than at West School?

○ 256
○ 254
○ 246
○ 244

Understand Plan Solve Check

Model 3-Digit Subtraction: Regroup Hundreds

Solve.

1. Mr. Smith drives 865 miles in May. He drives 683 miles in June. How many more miles does he drive in May than in June?

   _182_ more miles

2. Judy lives 428 miles from Rick's house and 349 miles from Bill's house. How many more miles does she live from Rick's house than from Bill's house?

   _____ more miles

3. Ms. Marvin drives 115 miles on Monday and 204 miles on Tuesday. How many more miles does she drive on Tuesday than on Monday?

   _____ miles

4. Chuck drives 326 miles one week and 135 miles the next week. How many more miles does he drive in the first week than in the second?

   _____ miles

Mark the correct answer.

5. There were 952 children at the zoo. Then 526 children went home. How many children were left at the zoo?

   ○ 436

   ○ 434

   ○ 426

   ○ 424

6. There are 827 adults at the fair. There are 441 children. How many more adults than children are there?

   ○ 426

   ○ 386

   ○ 326

   ○ 317

Reading Strategy • Sequence Events

Knowing the order in which things happen
can help you solve math problems.

Corey earns $4.50 doing chores.
Next he makes $2.35 raking leaves.
Then he spends $3.90.
How much money does Corey have left?

First Corey earns $4.50. Next
he makes $2.35. How much
does Corey make in all?

Corey makes __$6.85__.

$$\begin{array}{r} \$4.50 \\ + \ \$2.35 \\ \hline \$6.85 \end{array}$$

Then Corey spends $3.90.
How much money does he
have left?

Corey has __$2.95__.

$$\begin{array}{r} {}^{5\ \ 18} \\ \$6.85 \\ - \ \$3.90 \\ \hline \$2.95 \end{array}$$

Think about the order in which things happen. Then solve.

1. Ingrid has $5.50. She gets
   $2.75 for washing the dishes.
   Then she buys a doll for
   $6.15. How much money
   does Ingrid have left?

   _____

2. Ron buys a goldfish for $1.84
   and fish food for $1.97. He
   gives the clerk $5.01. How
   much change does Ron
   get back?

_____

(Understand) (Plan) (Solve) (Check)

Addition and Multiplication

Complete the addition sentence. Then complete the multiplication sentence.

1. There are 2 nests. There are 4 eggs in each nest. How many eggs are there?

$$\underline{4} + \underline{4} = \underline{8} \qquad \underline{2} \times \underline{4} = \underline{8}$$

---

2. There are 3 trees. There are 4 birds in each tree. How many birds are there?

$$\underline{\quad} + \underline{\quad} + \underline{\quad} = \underline{\quad} \qquad \underline{\quad} \times \underline{\quad} = \underline{\quad}$$

---

3. There are 5 balls. There are 2 black stripes on each ball. How many black stripes are there?

$$\underline{\ } + \underline{\ } + \underline{\ } + \underline{\ } + \underline{\ } = \underline{\ } \qquad \underline{\quad} \times \underline{\quad} = \underline{\quad}$$

Mark the correct answer.

4. Which number sentence matches the picture?

○ $2 + 5 = 7$

○ $2 \times 5 = 10$

○ $5 \times 5 = 25$

5. Which number sentence matches the picture?

○ $3 \times 3 = 9$

○ $5 \times 3 = 15$

○ $5 \times 5 = 25$

Name _____

Arrays

Solve. Draw a picture to show your work.

1. Mary plants 2 rows of flowers.
   She plants 8 flowers in each row.
   How many flowers does Mary plant?

   _____ × _____ = _____

   Mary plants _____ flowers.

2. Marcel puts his toy cars in 4 rows.
   There are 3 cars in each row. How
   many toy cars does Marcel have?

   _____ × _____ = _____

   Marcel has _____ toy cars.

3. Mr. Díaz puts the desks in 5 rows.
   There are 3 desks in each row.
   How many desks are there in all?

   _____ × _____ = _____

   There are _____ desks.

Mark the correct answer.

4. 2 rows
   10 in each row

   ○ $2 \times 5 = 10$

   ○ $2 + 10 = 12$

   ○ $2 \times 10 = 20$

   ○ $20 + 20 = 40$

5. 3 rows
   6 in each row

   ○ $3 \times 2 = 6$

   ○ $6 + 3 = 9$

   ○ $3 \times 5 = 15$

   ○ $3 \times 6 = 18$

PS160 **Problem Solving**

Understand   Plan   Solve   Check

Multiply in Any Order

Solve. Write the multiplication sentence two different ways.

1. Kira makes 3 rows of cards. Each row has 4 cards in it. How many cards are there in all?

___ × ___ = ___

___ × ___ = ___

Kira has ___ cards.

2. Ben has 9 marbles. He buys 9 more. How many marbles does Ben have now?

___ × ___ = ___

___ × ___ = ___

Ben has ___ marbles.

3. Destiny sorts her pictures into 4 piles. Each pile has 8 pictures. How many pictures does Destiny have in all?

___ × ___ = ___

___ × ___ = ___

Destiny has ___ pictures.

4. Dan makes 5 fruit baskets. He puts 3 oranges in each basket. How many oranges does Dan use in all?

___ × ___ = ___

___ × ___ = ___

Dan used ___ oranges.

Mark the correct answer.

5. What is another way to write $5 \times 2 = 10$?

○ $5 + 2 = 7$

○ $2 + 5 = 7$

○ $2 \times 5 = 10$

○ $10 \times 2 = 20$

6. What is another way to write $3 \times 2 = 6$?

○ $2 \times 3 = 6$

○ $3 + 2 = 5$

○ $3 \times 6 = 18$

○ $6 \times 2 = 12$

Equal Groups: Size of Groups

Use ●. Solve.

---

1. There are 15 children in the swim club. There are 3 equal teams. How many children are on each team?

_____**5**_____ children

2. There are 20 children in music class. The teacher divides the class into 5 equal groups. How many children are in each group?

_____ children

---

3. There are 8 baseball teams. The teams divide evenly to play on 4 fields. How many teams play on each field?

_____ teams

4. There are 18 baseball players. There are 2 equal teams. How many players are on each team?

_____ players

Mark the correct answer.

5. Susan has 6 baseballs. She puts the same number of balls in each of 2 bags. How many balls does she put in each bag?

○ 2

○ 3

○ 6

○ 12

6. David has 12 baseball cards. He puts the same number of cards on each page of his album. He fills 3 pages. How many cards does he put on each page?

○ 2

○ 3

○ 4

○ 12

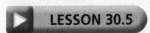

Understand Plan Solve Check

Equal Groups: Number of Groups

Solve. Draw a picture to help.

1. There are 8 books and 3 children. Each child gets the same number of books. How many books are left over?

   Each child gets _____ books.

   _____ books left over

2. There are 12 stickers and 3 children. Each child gets the same number of stickers. How many stickers are left over?

   Each child gets _____ stickers.

   _____ stickers left over

3. There are 11 balloons and 4 children. Each child gets the same number of balloons. How many balloons are left over?

   Each child gets _____ balloons.

   _____ balloons left over

Mark the correct answer.

4. There are 5 flowers and 2 children. Each child gets 2 flowers. How many flowers are left over?

   ○ 1   ○ 2
   ○ 3   ○ 4

5. There are 15 dolls and 4 children. Each child gets 3 dolls. How many dolls are left over?

   ○ 1   ○ 2
   ○ 3   ○ 4

Name _____

Understand   Plan   Solve   Check

Reading Strategy • Retell the Story

Sometimes retelling a problem in your own words can help you solve it.

Eileen has 15 pieces of chalk. The numbers of yellow, blue, and purple pieces are equal. How many pieces of chalk are there of each color?

Retell the problem.

Eileen has ___15___ pieces of chalk.

There are ___3___ different colors.

How many pieces of each color are there?

There are ___5___ pieces of each color.

Retell the problem in your own words. Then solve.

1. Jim has 12 building blocks. The numbers of red, green, and yellow blocks are equal. How many blocks of each color are there?

   _____ blocks of each color

2. Anita has 9 pieces of fruit. The numbers of apples, oranges, and bananas are equal. How many of each kind of fruit are there?

   _____ of each fruit